D0031144

Alice Munro

MANCHESTER
UNIVERSITY PRESS

CONTEMPORARY WORLD WRITERS

SERIES EDITOR   JOHN THIEME

ALREADY PUBLISHED IN THE SERIES

Peter Carey   BRUCE WOODCOCK
Toni Morrison   JILL MATUS
Salman Rushdie   CATHERINE CUNDY

FORTHCOMING

Anita Desai   SHIRLEY CHEW
Kazuo Ishiguro   BARRY LEWIS
Hanif Kureishi   BART MOORE-GILBERT
Ngugi wa Thiong'o   PATRICK WILLIAMS
Timothy Mo   ELAINE YEE LIN HO
Les Murray   STEVEN MATTHEWS
Caryl Phillips   BENEDICTE LEDENT
Wole Soyinka   ABDULRAZAK GURNAH
Derek Walcott   JOHN THIEME

Alice Munro

CORAL ANN HOWELLS

Manchester University Press

Manchester and New York

distributed exclusively in the USA by St. Martin's Press

The right of Coral Ann Howells to be identified as the author of this work has been asserted by her in accordance with the Copyright, Designs and Patents Act 1988.

Published by Manchester University Press
Oxford Road, Manchester M13 9NR, UK
and Room 400, 175 Fifth Avenue, New York, NY 10010, USA

Distributed exclusively in the USA by
St. Martin's Press, Inc. 175 Fifth Avenue, New York, NY 10010, USA

Distributed exclusively in Canada by
UBC Press, University of British Columbia, 6344 Memorial Road, Vancouver, BC, Canada V6T 1Z2

British Library Cataloguing-in-Publication Data
A catalogue record for this book is available from the British Library

Library of Congress Cataloging-in-Publication Data
Howells, Coral Ann.
    Alice Munro / Coral Ann Howells
        p.   cm. — (Contemporary world writers)
    Includes bibliographical references and index.
    ISBN 0-7190-4558-4 (hardcover). — ISBN 0-7190-4559-2 (pbk.)
    1. Munro, Alice—Criticism and interpretation. 2. Women and literature—Canada—History—20th century. I. Title. II. Series.
PR9199.3.M8Z7 1998   98-18302
813'.54—dc21

ISBN 0 7190 4558 4 *hardback*
    0 7190 4559 2 *paperback*

First published 1998
05   04   03   02   01   00   99   98   10 9 8 7 6 5 4 3 2 1

Typeset in Aldus
by Koinonia, Manchester
Printed in Great Britain
by Bell & Bain Limited, Glasgow

For Linda Marshall and Paula Bourne,
in love and friendship

Contents

Acknowledgements

Alice Munro's stories have fascinated me since the early 1980s when I first read them at the University of Guelph, Ontario, close to her home place. Since then I have been reading and writing and talking about Munro both in Britain and on frequent visits to Canada, and my thanks to the many people who have generously assisted in my research for this book might be laid out like a map – Guelph: to Linda and Leslie Marshall, especially for our visits to Wingham, Clinton and Goderich, to Ajay Heble, Donna Palmateer Pennee, J.R. (Tim) Struthers, Mary Swan and Paul Stack, Research Librarian at the University of Guelph; Wingham: to Mabel Jackson, Curator of Wingham and District Museum; Goderich: to Patricia Hamilton, Huron County Museum, and to Dennis and Mary Ann Duffy who from a distance have provided valuable information about a nine-teenth-century Goderich poetess, and more recently about a new Munro short story; Toronto: to Paula and Larry Bourne, and to Frieda Forman, Librarian of the Women's Resource Centre at OISE (Ontario Institute for Studies in Education), University of Toronto; Calgary: to Apollonia L. Steele who generously made Alice Munro manuscript materials in the University of Calgary Archives available to me, both on site and on the world wide web. And on this side of the Atlantic, my gratitude to Tom French of the British Library, Carole Robb of the University of Reading English Department, Gaynor Davies of Reading University Library and Robin Clifford, all of whom helped me to find my way through the mysteries of the web and CD-Roms. My thanks to the British Association for Canadian Studies, the Foundation for Canadian Studies in the United Kingdom and the University of Reading Research Board for travel assistance on my visits to Canada, and to the Department of English at Reading for a research term during which I was able to write a substantial part of this book. I would also like to thank the students in my Canadian Women's Writing classes at Reading for their enthusiasm and insightful critical comments. Thanks to John Thieme, General Editor of this series, for his wise and friendly editorial advice. And closest to home, my thanks as always to Robin, Phoebe and Miranda.

I am grateful to the following for permission to reprint, in whole or in part, material which has been previously published: to Königshausen and Neumann (Wurzburg) for permission to reprint 'Alice Munro's art of indeterminacy: *The Progress of Love*' from R. Nischik and B. Korte (eds), *Modes of Narrative* (1990), 41–52; to Rodopi (Amsterdam) for permission to reprint 'Taking Risks: Alice Munro's "The Jack Randa Hotel"' from H. Maes-Jelinek, G. Collier and G. V. Davis (eds), *A Talent(ed) Digger* (1996), 387–93, and to Liège Language and Literature (Liège University) for permission to reprint 'Star Maps and shifting perspectives: Alice Munro's *The Moons of Jupiter*' from G. Debusscher and M. Maufort (eds), *Union in Partition* (1997), 173–80.

Series editor's foreword

Contemporary World Writers is an innovative series of authoritative introductions to a range of culturally diverse contemporary writers from outside Britain and the United States, or from 'minority' backgrounds within Britain or the United States. In addition to providing comprehensive general introductions, books in the series also argue stimulating original theses, often but not always related to contemporary debates in postcolonial studies.

The series locates individual writers within their specific cultural contexts, while recognising that such contexts are themselves invariably a complex mixture of hybridised influences. It aims to counter tendencies to appropriate the writers discussed into the canon of English or American literature or to regard them as 'other'.

Each volume includes a chronology of the writer's life, an introductory section on formative contexts and intertexts, discussion of all the writer's major works, a bibliography of primary and secondary works and an index. Issues of racial, national and cultural identity are explored, as are gender and sexuality. Books in the series also examine writers' use of genre, particularly ways in which Western genres are adapted or subverted and 'traditional' local forms are reworked in a contemporary context.

Contemporary World Writers aims to bring together the theoretical impulse which currently dominates postcolonial studies and closely argued readings of particular authors' works, and by so doing to avoid the danger of appropriating the specifics of particular texts into the hegemony of totalising theories.

List of abbreviations

Chronology

1931   Alice Ann Laidlaw born 10 July in Wingham, Ontario. Her father Robert Laidlaw was a fox farmer and her mother Anne a former schoolteacher; the eldest of three children.

1937   Starts primary school at Lower Town School, Wingham.

1939   Outbreak of World War 2; begins attending Wingham Public School.

1943   Mother suffering from illness later to be diagnosed as Parkinson's Disease.

1944–48   Attends Wingham and District High School where in her final year she receives Dominion Provincial Bursary and Whyte Memorial Scholarship for French; fox farm fails, father becomes night watchman at Wingham Foundry and later begins turkey farming.

1949-51   Attends University of Western Ontario on a two-year scholarship, where she reads journalism then changes to English; works part-time in public library; her first short story 'The Dimensions of a Shadow' is published in student literary magazine *Folio*.

1951   Marries James Armstrong Munro and moves to Vancouver.

1953   Sheila, her first daughter is born; sells first short story 'A Basket of Strawberries' to *Mayfair* magazine.

1954–57   'The Strangers' is sold to Robert Weaver for CBC Trans Canada Matinée radio programme. In 1950s and 1960s publishes short stories regularly in *Chatelaine, The Tamarack Review, Canadian Forum, The Montrealer, Queen's Quarterly*; second daughter Jenny is born.

1959   Mother dies from Parkinson's Disease; Alice writes 'The Peace of Utrecht' that summer, which is published in 1960 in *The Tamarack Review*.

1963–66   Alice, husband and family move to Victoria, B.C. where they run a bookshop Munro's Books; Andrea, third daughter, is born.

1968   First short story collection *Dance of the Happy Shades* published; wins Governor General's Award for fiction.

1971   *Lives of Girls and Women* published; wins Canadian Booksellers' Award.

1973   Marriage breaks up; Alice moves to Nelson B.C. to teach creative writing, then to London, Ontario, with two younger daughters; teaches creative writing at York University in Toronto.

1974   *Something I've Been Meaning to Tell You* published; writer in residence at her old university of Western Ontario.

1975–76   Moves to Clinton, Ontario, 20 miles from Wingham, where she lives with and then marries Gerald Fremlin, a geographer whom she knew as a student at Western; father dies in Toronto hospital after a heart operation; begins selling stories to *The New Yorker*; awarded honorary Doctorate of Letters from University of Western Ontario.

1977–78   *Who Do You Think You Are?* published; wins Governor General's Award. Published in Britain and USA as *The Beggar Maid*, shortlisted for the Booker Prize; her screen play *1847: The Irish* is broadcast in CBC Television series *The Newcomers/Les Arrivants*.

1979   Visit to Australia as winner of Canada–Australia Literary Prize (1978); Robert Laidlaw's novel *The McGregors: A Novel of an Ontario Pioneer Family* published posthumously.

1980   Writer in residence at University of British Columbia, Vancouver and then at University of Queensland, Brisbane, Australia.

1981   Visit to China with Group of Seven Canadian Writers, where she celebrates her 50th birthday in Guangzhou.

1982   *Moons of Jupiter* published; book promotion tour of Scandinavia; first academic conference on Alice Munro is held at University of Waterloo, Ontario.

1986   *The Progress of Love* published; wins Governor General's Award and Marian Engel Award.

1990–91   *Friend of My Youth* published; shortlisted for Governor General's Award; wins Ontario Trillium Book Award, Commonwealth Writers' Prize (Canada and Caribbean Region); awarded the Canada Council Molson Prize for 'outstanding contribution to the cultural and intellectual life of Canada'; becomes a grandmother for the first time.

1994   *Open Secrets* published; wins W. H. Smith Award in 1995; 'What Do You Want to Know For?' published in *Writing Away: The PEN Canada Travel Anthology*.

1996   *Alice Munro: Selected Stories* published; 'The Love of a Good Woman' published in *The New Yorker* in December Double Fiction Issue.

1997   'The Children Stay' published in *The New Yorker* in December Double Fiction Issue.

1998   'Jakarta' published in *Saturday Night* in February issue.

1998   *The Love of a Good Woman* published.

Everybody knows what a house does, how it encloses space and makes connections between one enclosed space and another and presents what is outside in a new way. This is the nearest I can come to explaining what a story does for me, and what I want my stories to do for other people.

('What Is Real?')

The corn in tassel, the height of summer passing, time opening out with room for ordinary anxieties, weariness, tiffs, triviality ... Back where nothing seems to be happening, beyond the change of seasons.

('What Do You Want to Know For?')

Contexts and intertexts

Is it true that in order to appreciate Alice Munro's stories we need to begin by looking at a map of Canada? Certainly the fictions of Canada's greatest short story writer are tied to specific geographical locations, for Munro is fascinated by local history and geography and her stories offer social maps of small-town life in rural Ontario, though like women's gossip they also retail socially unspeakable events, those 'Open Secrets' which she insists on telling and which are definitely off the map. To read Munro's stories is to discover the delights of seeing two worlds at once: an ordinary everyday world and the shadowy map of another imaginary or secret world laid over the real one, so that in reading we slip from one world into the other in an unassuming domestic sort of way. Where but in Munro would we find a sentence like this:

> So my father drives and my brother watches the road for rabbits and I feel my father's life flowing back from our car in the last of the afternoon, darkening and turning strange, like a landscape that has an enchantment on it, making it kindly, ordinary and familiar while you are looking at it, but changing it, once your back is turned, into something you will never know, with all kinds of weathers, and distances you cannot imagine.[1]

This description by a young girl of the imaginative process of transformation from 'touchable' into 'mysterious' might also be taken as Munro's description of her own quality of vision and of her fictional method of mapping alternative worlds.

Munro writes about the places she knows best, the area where she grew up in the 1930s and 1940s and where she still lives. To return to that map of Canada, if we began by locating a group of small towns in southwestern Ontario (Wingham, Clinton and Goderich on Lake Huron) we would delineate Munro's geographical territory. Though her stories make some excursions outside to Toronto and to Vancouver, and later to Australia and Scotland and even Albania, her work is situated within a long tradition of Canadian small-town fiction where anywhere else is outside and alien, be it as near as Toronto or as far away as Sydney, Australia. Munro left her home town when she went to university in London, Ontario a few hours' bus ride away; then she married and went to live in British Columbia for twenty years where her three children were born and where she and her husband ran a bookshop in Victoria. Of that life she writes, 'All through the 50s I was living in a dormitory suburb, having babies, and writing wasn't part of the accepted thing for a girl or a woman to do at that time either, but it never occurred to me that I should stop.'[2] Significantly, Munro emphasises the fact that she had gone on writing stories all through that period and twenty-one were published before her first collection *Dance of the Happy Shades* appeared in 1968, when it won the prestigious Governor General's Award. Her first two books appeared while she was in British Columbia, then in the early 1970s she separated from her husband and returned to Ontario where she remarried and still lives, in a town not far from where she grew up. With her increasing international reputation she began to travel to England and Scotland, then to Australia in 1979 and 1980, and she spent her fiftieth birthday in China with a group of Canadian writers. These travel experiences are reflected in an occasional widening of reference in her stories from *The Moons of Jupiter* onwards, though the Ontario small-town rural community remains her ground base.

Not surprisingly, Munro has often been asked whether her stories are autobiographical, to which she has replied: 'In incident, no ... in emotion, completely.'[3] The answer would seem to be rather more confusing ('Lots of true answers are') as she reveals in her 1982 essay 'What Is Real?' where she tried to explain how she writes a story:

> Some of the material I may have lying around already, in memories and observations, and some I invent, and some I have to go diligently looking for (factual details), while some is dumped in my lap (anecdotes and bits of speech). I see how this material might go together to make the shape I need, and I try it.[4]

In her third collection there is a story called 'Material' which takes this commentary on the relation between real life and fiction a stage further, telling the story of an unfortunate woman called Dotty in Vancouver, from the contrasting perspectives of a male and a female writer.

How is it that these stories travel so well and appeal, as they strongly do, to an international readership? Do readers outside Canada read them for the ways in which the lives they represent look different from our own lives or for the ways in which they seem familiar? Indeed the people of Wingham do not much like her stories (they tend to regard them as scandalous gossip), and there is nothing about Munro in either the local museum in Wingham or the Huron County Museum in Goderich. Of course it is precisely Munro's documentary quality which is the secret of her international appeal, for readers know where we are (or think we do) because she creates locations and characters so exactly. Yet at the same time, these stories could be anywhere – any small town, any farmhouse:

> A lot of people think I'm a regional writer. And I use the region where I grew up a lot. But I don't have any idea of writing to show the kind of things that happen in a certain place. These things happen and the place is part of it. But in a way it's incidental.[5]

Her female narrators all have a fine double awareness of community values and of what else goes on outside those limits. They are fascinated by dark holes and by unscripted spaces with their scandalous discreditable stories of transgression and desire. Munro registers this doubleness of vision very clearly in *Lives of Girls and Women* when describing her adolescent narrator's home town of Jubilee: 'People's lives in Jubilee, as elsewhere, were dull, simple, amazing, unfathomable, deep caves paved with kitchen linoleum.'[6] Such perception exposes the limits of realistic fiction by its challenge to domestic surfaces, hinting at what is usually hidden or unspoken within the acknowledged order of small-town social life. Munro's stories are frequently introduced as gossip and they circulate as gossip; they are complicated interwoven fragments, full of glimpses of parallel lives and silent female knowledge – of women's bodies and the many 'casualties of the female life', of love stories and failed romantic fantasies, also of adolescent girls' aspirations for more glamorous narratives than their everyday lives contain. Munro takes up the traditional subjects of women's fiction, acknow-ledging their imaginative appeal and power, though her stories significantly alter female plots so that they become stories of entrapment and escape with women seeing themselves as spies or aliens, and where secrecy and silence are strategies of camouflaged resistance to conventional social decorums. Again like gossip, these stories have a positive function as women's counter-discourse, suggesting alternative maps for women's destinies beyond traditional patterns of male authority and gender stereotyping, sketching new ways to represent women's differences – not only from men but also from one another across gaps of generation, class and education.

In order to highlight what I consider the most significant issues in Munro's fiction I propose to develop the imagery of maps and mapping which is so popular in contemporary feminist criticism and postcolonial writing and which happens to be peculiarly appropriate for Munro. Munro uses cartography as a device which allows her stories of the multiple lives in small towns to be told, while Del Jordan's map which she traces on a dead cow's hide the day of her uncle's funeral has become emblematic for many feminist critics of the woman writer's concern to chart alternative spaces and to mark new positions from which to speak:

> Tracing the outline of a continent again, digging the stick
> in, trying to make a definite line, I paid attention to its
> shape as I would sometimes pay attention to the shape of
> real continents or islands on real maps, as if the shape
> itself were a revelation beyond words, and I would be able
> to make sense of it, if I tried hard enough, and had time.
> (*LGW*, 45) [7]

The point about maps is that they chart locations of things in
relationship to one another, providing a visual and spatial
understanding of places, events or processes. Maps are a way of
representing not only topographical features but also social
geography and historical records through buried maps of a
community's past, while they may also be used as metaphors to
illustrate relationships between inner psychological spaces and
the outside world. In Munro's projects of textual mapping,
alternative worlds are positioned alongside in the same
geographical and fictional space so that realistic street maps of
small towns are overlaid or undermined by maps of characters'
inner lives and by memory maps of nearly forgotten family or
local history – as if the everyday might be transformed to reveal
'the other side of dailiness'[8] if we just paid attention and looked
closely enough. These stories make readers see that there is
always something else which is out there unmapped, still
'floating around loose' or partially figured in myths and fantasy
and the wheeling constellations of the stars.

It is this alternative mapping which codes in elements of
experience not otherwise representable within realistic fiction
which is the link with Munro's treatment of women's romantic
fantasies, the other feature which I wish to highlight as insistently
present in her fiction from the beginning.[9] As a woman writer
Munro is always aware of girls and women as thinking, feeling
beings located within their female bodies, for she emphasises
that female subjectivity is intimately bound up with sexuality
and desire, and the contradictoriness of women's desires is one
of her major topics.[10] Munro is not a feminist theorist though
the work of Luce Irigaray and Rosi Braidotti in particular offer
some fascinating perspectives through which to interpret her

fiction.[11] Instead, she provides the bewildering experiential evidence with which theorists are seeking to come to terms as she explores sexual difference from within – in women's fantasies and in the dynamic relations between women and men as well as between women themselves. Since the early 1980s there has been a lot of critical attention paid to popular romances and to women's romantic fantasies, and Munro's fiction like Margaret Atwood's seems to be crucial in delineating this central area of female subjectivity.[12] As she says of her adolescent heroine Del Jordan, 'Del was sabotaged by love – all women are'[13] and her stories present endless celebrations and revisions of female romantic fantasies with all their urgent eroticism, their bewildering contradictions and disappointments, and their defiance of age and experience. She does not write Harlequin romances or soft porn though she understands precisely their appeal, as the female narrator of 'Bardon Bus' notes with some self irony:

> The images, the language, of pornography and romance are alike; monotonous and mechanically seductive, quickly leading to despair. That was what my mind dealt in; that is what it still can deal in. I have tried vigilance and reading serious books but I can still slide deep into some scene before I know where I am.[14]

The raw material of the psyche is the same, as that narrator reminds us: 'I can't apologize for the banality of my dreams' (*MJ*, 127). Romantic fantasy provides escape though it is not merely about escapism; nor is it simply a 'how-to book for women who lack power' though that access to power through love and sex is important too.[15] Such fantasy also provides an inner space from which to imagine alternative life stories and to renegotiate connections, at least in imagination, between private and public worlds. This is the secret world where women make discoveries about their deepest desires and fears, and only here do Munro's protagonists penetrate some of the mysteries within which they must work out their lives and personal relationships. Their fantasies dramatise women's parallel unlived lives of dreamed-of possibilities, culminating in a late story like 'Carried Away' in

Open Secrets where an old woman meets the ghost of a man who has been dead for years and he declares his love for her in a hallucinatory moment of 'radiant vanishing consolations'.[16] But for all their shimmering promises, fantasies always turn out to be 'unreliable structures' 'rickety inventions' or 'sudden holes and impromptu tricks'. They are untrustworthy but they are also infinitely seductive because they offer at least partial maps of the feminine imaginary.

For Munro writing belongs to the same realm: 'You come to writing with total faith that it is going to transform life in a way so dazzling that this is the total end of your life ... Not so.'[17] Interestingly, comments such as this elide the difference between romantic fantasy and the creative writing process, for both activities include imaginative transformations and the delights of anticipation. In a 1982 interview she spoke about the initial rush of excitement before beginning to write a story, 'When it hits me ... I think that beginning perception, that first perception, is the total moment, and from then on there's all this work.'[18] In her story 'White Dump' she makes a parallel comment about a love affair: 'I think the best part is always right at the beginning ... Perhaps just when it flashes on you what's possible. That may be the best.'[19] In a similar way Munro, a reading addict from the age of nine, describes reading as a kind of falling in love and writing as its necessary sequel:

> With a story that I loved, I would go back and read it over and over again. It was a desire for possession. I guess it was like being in love. I could not possess it *enough*, so I made up my own story that was like it. All through high school, I made up a fake *Wuthering Heights*. Before that I was making my own imitations of the poetry [Tennyson] and before that of the historical novel [Charles Dickens's *A Child's History of England].*[20]

There are traces of Munro's reading in what her protagonists read, and especially in *Lives of Girls and Women* where Del Jordan too reads Tennyson's poems and *Wuthering Heights* as well as the *Encyclopaedia Britannica* which her mother is peddling around the Ontario countryside in the late 1940s. In many interviews Munro has recalled not only her early delight in the forbidden pleasures of reading ('There were stories in my community about women who had become readers, in the way that they might take up drinking')[21] but also the books which mattered most to her. Of those the two most important were both by women. She read L. M. Montgomery's *Emily of New Moon*, 'the watershed book of my life' when she was nine or ten and wrote an Afterword to it for the New Canadian Library edition in 1989, still trying to account for its appeal. Of course there would have been an obvious attraction because it is the story of a small-town girl enraptured by language who decides to become a writer and for whom 'reading and writing are the first romances of her life'.[22] Yet there is something else as well: 'In this book, as in all the books I've loved, there's so much going on behind, or beyond, the proper story. There's life spreading out behind the story – the book's life – and we see it out of the corner of the eye.'[23] So it is with *Wuthering Heights*, 'the next great, great book, which I read when I was fourteen'.[24] Not only does Munro see it as 'the ancestor of all the romances with the strong brutal hero' and having the same kind of appeal as Margaret Mitchell's best-seller *Gone with the Wind* (1936) which she was reading in the same period, but there is also a fascination with Brontë's landscape and what she calls 'density about place that transcends the story completely'.[25] Directions are already signalled here, with Munro's interest in the imaginative transformations of ordinariness and in women's regional fiction. This may come from Yorkshire, the American South or the Maritimes, though in her youth Munro had no particular feeling for Canada: 'Prince Edward Island [the setting for Montgomery's novels] was as remote to me as Maine would have been.'[26] Though Munro continued to read 'anything and everything' it is her adult interest in the female literary tradition that I wish to highlight, notably her interest during the 1950s in women writers of the American South like Eudora Welty, Carson McCullers and Flannery O'Connor, where she 'felt there a country being depicted that was like my own … I mean, the part of the country I come from is absolutely

Gothic.'[27] I believe that Munro learned a great deal from Welty's stories in *The Golden Apples* which she read and reread when it appeared in 1949, and I shall explore their affinity of vision in my discussion of 'Dance of the Happy Shades' in comparison with Welty's 'June Recital'. Robert Thacker has drawn attention to her later interest in Willa Cather's stories, reminding readers that the librarian in 'Carried Away' lists Cather as one of her favourite authors in 1917, and that Munro's story 'Dulse' which is set near Cather's cottage on Grand Manan Island, New Brunswick, is a 'complex invocation and meditation upon Cather'.[28] Such a detailed documentary history of intertextual encounters suggests the crucial importance to Munro of reading and writing fiction as one of the few ways for a young woman living on the outskirts of Wingham to evade the constraints of small-town life and to gain a sense of power:

> When I was about fifteen I made the glorious leap from being a victim of my own ... self conscious miseries to being a godlike arranger of patterns and destinies, even if they were all in my head; I have never leapt back.[29]

Instead of leaping back, Munro has continued to experiment with the short story form, always attempting to represent more adequately the complex layering of the way things are or rather the ways things might be interpreted from different perspectives. Her stories enact the process of trying to make sense out of what happens, though as she remarked on the publication of *Open Secrets*, 'The older I get [she is sixty-six] the more I see things as having more than one explanation.'[30] While she insistently refuses to theorise about short stories she has on occasions attempted to explain what a story 'does', either via the famous 'House' metaphor which I quote at the beginning about enclosing spaces and making connections, or via metafictional comments within her stories about 'shifts of emphasis which throw the storyline open to question'[31] or 'structural treacheries'.[32] Commenting on *Open Secrets* (which she does not see as a good introduction to her work) she says:

It seems as if I want to get a lot of layers going. I want the
story to have a lot of levels, so that the reader can draw
back and perhaps instead of thinking about what happens
in this story as far as development of plot goes, to think of
something else about life … This may be a difficult way to
write fiction.[33]

At the end of 1996 Munro's *Selected Stories* appeared – twenty-
eight of them – all published previously and chosen by Munro in
consultation with her Canadian and American publishers, to
represent her *œuvre* chronologically but with a rearrangement
of the order of stories within each collection. Possibly as the
review in *Books in Canada* suggests, 'we have to read this as a
new presentation in itself, as a narrative on its own, and as a
defence of her art',[34] although it seems to me unlikely that any
narrative of Munro's could exist on its own. The rearrangements within *Selected Stories* would seem to be another example
of those characteristic 'shifts of emphasis which throw the
storyline open to question' and another statement of Munro's
rejection of single or closed meanings in favour of significations
which continually shift when events are viewed from different
angles.

Certainly Munro's narrative methods have changed over
thirty years, as she allows more and more possible meanings to
circulate in every story while refusing definitive interpretations
or plot resolutions. I shall briefly summarise the changes which
I shall discuss in the following chapters. In the early collections
and whole book story sequences up to *The Beggar Maid* (1978)[35]
Munro works within the tradition of documentary realism,
registering surface details of daily life and then disrupting those
realistic conventions by shifts into fantasy, suggesting alternative worlds that coexist within the same fictional space.
Endings are a significant feature in many of these stories, where
something extra is added – some insight or additional detail of
information – which unsettles the carefully constructed narrative. I have referred to this as a principle of supplementarity,
following Derrida's concept of the 'unsettling supplement' as a
feature not only of the play of language but of narrative itself.[36]

The major shift in her storytelling methods in the 1980s, which I identify with *The Moons of Jupiter* and *The Progress of Love*, is an amplification of this principle. Instead of placing the supplement at the end, supplementarity pervades the whole narrative through time shifts and shifts in narrative perspective, unsettling the story at every stage of its telling. The story becomes a series of 'arrangements, disarrangements and earnest deceptions'[37] where multiple and often contradictory meanings have room to circulate in structures of narrative indeterminacy. Her two collections in the 1990s show Munro still engaged with the challenge of how to write stories that will adequately accommodate the indeterminacy and disparate realities observed by her increasingly self-conscious storytellers. Though they are still motivated like the adolescent Del Jordan to tell stories out of an impossible desire for wholeness and explanation ('every last thing, held still and held together' *LGW*, 249), they frequently come upon blankness and secrecy or fantasies and lies, whether they look closely into the present or take a long view over the past; the challenge is to be able to tell any story at all: 'She seems to be looking into an open secret, something not startling until you think of trying to tell it.'[38] Munro's stories are getting longer and longer and apparently more digressive with 'so many layers of things going on and crosscutting in time and memory.'[39] Ironically, although she has never written a 'proper novel' her short stories blur the distinction between genres, just as they celebrate both artifice and life by keeping multiple speculative meanings in circulation:

> I want the stories to keep going on. I want the story to exist somewhere so that in a way it's still happening, or happening over and over again. I don't want it to be shut up in the book and put away – oh well, that's what happened.[40]

The plan of this book is very simple. As indicated in the chapter headings, I shall discuss Munro's eight books in chronological sequence. In every collection I shall comment on the design of the volume while focussing discussion on three or four stories, aiming always for a double emphasis on thematic continuities and on Munro's ongoing experiments within the short story form and within small-town fiction, both of which are marks of her distinctive Canadian inheritance linking her in a tradition which goes back to nineteenth-century writers like Sara Jeanette Duncan and through into the twentieth with Stephen Leacock, Margaret Laurence, Robertson Davies and Isabel Huggan, for example. The only exception to this pattern is Chapter 2 where I treat two of the early collections together to counterbalance the two better known (and more frequently taught) whole book story sequences, *Lives of Girls and Women* and *The Beggar Maid*. I hope I have managed to imitate to some degree Munro's fictional maps with their surfaces and hidden depths and interconnections which never fail to surprise us by opening out into moments of radiance.

Ontario Gothic:
Dance of the Happy Shades and *Something I've Been Meaning to Tell You*

> The part of the country I come from is absolutely Gothic.
> You can't get it all down.[1]

SPEAKING about her fiction in the early 1970s Munro refers to its primary location in her home place of small-town southwestern Ontario, though what she emphasises is not its familiarity but its strangeness. This is a place so full of mysteries and secrets that even the most meticulous documentation may fail to net the complexities of small-town life and local history. The keyword here is 'Gothic': it contains the promise of melodramatic violence and buried lives; it also refers to Munro's affinity with women writers of the American South, especially Eudora Welty whose stories excited Munro so much in the 1950s, making it possible for her to imagine writing about the small-town communities and rural landscapes where she grew up. As Munro says, 'It's a matter of vision' where North American women writing a thousand miles apart (in Mississippi and Ontario) share a similar vision of place and of people's relation to their place as if there are always multiple worlds to be charted, so that the small towns in their fiction become paradoxically both 'touchable and mysterious'. In this Chapter I shall discuss Munro's two early short story collections where she first learned her craft and where she marks out her fictional territory and her distinctively feminine perspective as a storyteller.

The stories in *Dance of the Happy Shades* written over a period of fifteen years show the experimental quality of her writing during the 1950s and 1960s, and more excitingly the

breakthrough moment when she found her distinctive voice in
the summer of 1959 with 'The Peace of Utrecht' and 'Dance of
the Happy Shades':

> 'The Peace of Utrecht' was the story where I first tackled
> personal material. It was the first story I absolutely had to
> write and wasn't writing to see if I could write that kind of
> story. I think every young writer starts out this way ...
> But when a story takes over the way that one did with me,
> then you see, then *I* saw, that writing was about
> something else altogether than I had suspected it was, that
> it was going to be less in my control and more inescapable
> than I had thought.[2]

If Munro discovered her voice with *Dance of the Happy Shades*,
she only discovered her genre with *Something I've Been Meaning
to Tell You*:

> And yet, I think the most attractive kind of writing of all is
> just the single story. It satisfies me the way nothing else
> does ... For years and years I would convince myself that I
> really had a novel there and I would take these ideas I had
> and bloat them up and I would start writing them and they
> would go all – they would just fall. It was just a total waste
> of time ... So it took me a long time to reconcile myself to
> being a short story writer.[3]

That word 'bloat' conveys Munro's judgement on her novel-
writing attempts, and the fact that the title story of *Something
I've Been Meaning to Tell You* was based on a novel that she had
not managed to write would seem to signal her own recognition
of the decisive shift of genre. The collection of single stories with
no definitive narrative implications in their arrangement becomes
the model for Munro's work (with the exception of *Lives of
Girls and Women* and *The Beggar Maid*) and though it is true
that the design of every book encourages the reader to make
connections, such shadowy parallels and correspondences are
artificial and at best very provisional constructions which do not
detract from individual narratives in all their variety.

Following a similarly loose arrangement, I have selected
five stories (three from *Dance of the Happy Shades* and two from

Something I've Been Meaning to Tell You) which illustrate Munro's distinctive textual mapping of landscape and her feminine mode of storytelling as gossip – a comparison she makes herself in one of these stories when her narrator talks about using real people as fictional characters to 'suit her purposes':

> Though I am only doing in a large and public way what has always been done, what my mother did, and other people did, who mentioned to me my grandmother's story. Even in that close-mouthed place, stories were being made. People carried their stories around with them. My grandmother carried hers, and nobody ever spoke of it to her face.[4]

Indeed, these stories perform similar functions to gossip for not only do they give their narrators a kind of power to cope with circumstances which they probably cannot change but they also strive to make sense out of the randomness and confusion of everyday life. 'Walker Brothers Cowboy' and 'Dance of the Happy Shades' tell stories in the first person from a child's perspective as she begins to apprehend the secret worlds that exist on the periphery of the comfortable known world of home. 'The Peace of Utrecht' and 'The Ottawa Valley', told from a remembering adult's point of view, are her first attempts to represent the scandal of a mother's debilitating illness and death, while 'Something I've Been Meaning to Tell You' is an early version of Munro's ironical female romance plots, here given a sinisterly Gothic twist through one sister's lifelong jealousy of the other. Such a selection illustrates the variety of Munro's narrative experiments, told from a feminine perspective and bearing her characteristic mark of 'double vision'.[5] There is always the sense of ordinary surfaces covering over some secret or scandal which threatens to collapse them, and while Munro manages to contain the familiar and the unfamiliar within the same story structure, the realistic text is threatened by glimpses of a darker fantastic subtext which cannot be easily accommodated within the narrative. That Gothic world of desire and dread casts its gigantic shadows over the child's world in a story like 'Images' where the glimpse of the axeman coming silently through the bushes towards her father convinces her that 'our fears are based on nothing but the truth'.[6] Instinctively the child recognises the unspeakable nature of alternative realities, so that she feels like children in fairy tales, 'dazed and powerful with secrets, I never said a word' (DHS, 43). However the threats of violence and betrayal are usually hidden behind closed doors and the only time the word 'Gothic' explodes into the text is in 'The Peace of Utrecht' to describe a woman stricken with Parkinson's Disease when her daughters refer to her as 'our Gothic Mother' (DHS, 195). I have mapped my discussion in this Chapter on a principle of 'outside' and 'inside', using as my frame 'Walker Brothers Cowboy' and 'Dance of the Happy Shades', both of which are stories of being liberated into the undreamed-of spaces of imagination, and which enclose the darker secrets of 'The Peace of Utrecht' and 'Something I've Been Meaning to Tell You'. In addition, I shall treat 'The Ottawa Valley' which functions as a supplement to these; it is set outside southwestern Ontario and is explicitly autobiographical, yet as failed elegy for a dead mother it figures Munro's central dilemma of narrative representation.

With 'Walker Brothers Cowboy',[7] the first story in *Dance of the Happy Shades*, Munro signals the importance of geography and history in her fiction (as well as the importance of fathers). How is a place known? Munro's answer is to make maps of the landscape, presenting 'Tuppertown' an old grain port on Lake Huron from a child's perspective – or rather through an adult's memories of her 1930s childhood.[8] Told in the present tense, the story vividly records what a young girl sees when she goes out walking or driving with her father and her dawning perception of the multiple geographies hidden within her familiar world. It is Munro's earliest version of a feminist politics of location,[9] though instead of finding a position from which to speak, her young narrator is silenced by her newly awakened awareness of worlds hitherto unknown and unsuspected. The story is structured around a young girl's two adventures with her father. The first occurs on a summer evening when the two of them walk down to the park to look at Lake Huron, 'just to see if the Lake's still there' (*DHS*, 1), and the second when she and her younger brother drive out with him into the surrounding countryside, for he is a door-to-door salesman for the firm of Walker Brothers during the Depression in the 1930s. Simply structured on a binary pattern of centre and periphery, the story traces the topography of home and then radiates outwards tracing the child's efforts to comprehend layers of life beyond the orderly structures of her town's familiar street plan and family relationships.

The walk down to Lake Huron presents a scrupulously detailed map of the main street of Tuppertown with its old maple trees and people sitting out on the sidewalk in the evening, though the narrative emphasis is on 'leaving behind' such banalities as father and daughter turn towards the lake. Looking out over the water, he tells her about the origins of the Great Lakes at the end of the Ice Age, an archaeology of place which he figures by pressing his hand into the ground to illustrate the movement of the ice 'creeping down from the north'. We see the child's effort to imagine the strangeness of prehistory, 'before the Indians were there, before Tuppertown', though it is a strangeness from which she is protected by her father's presence. It is her father with his funny stories and jokes and his country-and-western songs who shows his daughter how to read the landscape for what is hidden in it, though he is an ambiguous guide who sometimes interprets for her and sometimes deliberately leaves things unexplained.

A similar ambiguity pervades the drive out into the country, where the two children and their father enter a rambling territory of dirt roads and tall unpainted farmhouses which is both familiar and strangely unfamiliar:

> The nineteen-thirties. How much this kind of farmhouse, this kind of afternoon, seem to me to belong to that one decade in time, just as my father's hat does, his bright flared tie, our car with its wide running board. (*DHS*, 8)

The journey charts all the markers of rural Depression landscape as the young girl notices 'the old cars, the pumps, dogs, views of grey barns and falling-down shed and unturning windmills' very much in the manner of the documentary photographers of the American South in the 1930s such as Walker Evans and Eudora Welty whose 'enormous' influence on her work Munro has frequently acknowledged.[10] Then the story shifts into more ambiguous areas as their father drives beyond his accustomed route to a place outside his sales territory, where a strange encounter occurs. He takes his children to visit his old girlfriend Nora Cronin, the woman whom he would have married if she had not been a Roman Catholic, and Munro almost incidentally reminds the reader of religious prejudice against Roman Catholics in Scots–Irish rural Ontario: 'So-and-so digs with the wrong foot, they would say' (DHS, 14). Despite the ordinary shabbiness of yet another unpainted house and the run-down farm where Nora lives with her blind old mother, the child is aware of something extraordinary about this visit, signalled in the woman's rapid change from 'dirty print smock and running shoes' into a showy floral afternoon dress. As she watches her father in Nora's company, laughing and drinking whisky ('One of the things my mother has told me in our talks together is that my father never drinks whisky,' DHS, 15) she is suddenly confronted with a new and unfamiliar vision of him. She senses though she cannot understand the emotional currents between the two adults, just as she hears below the conversational pleasantries the subtext of failed romance with its mutual longing and regret which can only be coded into Nora's flirt-atiousness and her father's polite refusals of any invitations to dance to the gramophone in the living room or to stay for supper. What she does register however is this woman's loneliness which seems to be on display, indeed written out for everyone to see as they drive away: 'She stands close to the car in her soft, brilliant dress. She touches the fender, making an unintelligible mark in the dust there' (DHS, 17). Nothing could more plainly signal the untranslatability of romantic fantasy than Nora's exotic dress and her scribbling in the dust. Though the story is firmly situated within the conventions of realism, such scrupulous attention to details reveals the 'other side of dailiness' where people's lives, as Del Jordan realises in *Lives of Girls and Women*, are not only 'dull and simple' but also 'amazing and unfathomable' (*LGW*, 249). We are witnessing the process of imaginative transformation where objects and events in the real world take on new significance within the subjective life of the storyteller. The child may have no language to describe the adult emotions she has witnessed, yet she perceives they are as alien to her own experience as the ancient history of the Great Lakes. So the story itself becomes a kind of subjective mapping of secret worlds into which the young girl has been initiated by her father, where she catches a glimpse of uncharted territory as fantastic and as awesome as any landscape out of fairytale, 'with all kinds of weathers, and distances you cannot imagine' (*DHS*, 18).

Turning from the unmapped open spaces associated by a daughter with her father, 'The Peace of Utrecht' for all its masculine overtones of wars and treaties focuses on domestic interiors and other kinds of battles within a web of female relationships between mothers and daughters and sisters and aunts.[11] This is home territory, but Munro takes us into the haunted house of a domestic horror story where two grown-up sisters are tormented by memories of their dead mother. Perhaps it is true that the archetypal Gothic plot with its key motifs of the 'unspeakable' and 'live burial' hinges on the absence or the death of the mother.[12] According to Luce Irigaray Western culture is founded not on parricide (as Freud hypothesised in *Totem and Taboo*) but on matricide and she warns daughters not to be accomplices in the murder of the mother: 'The relationship with the mother is a mad desire, because it is the dark continent, *par excellence*. It remains in the shadows of our culture; it is its night and its hell' – for daughters as well as for sons, with nothing but 'pain, screams and demands'.[13] It is this 'potentially deadly immediacy'[14] which is at the centre of Munro's story though masked by the rhythms of everyday life in a small town, when Helen the narrator returns home with her two children to Jubilee on a visit to her sister Maddy several months after their invalid mother's death: 'I have been at home now for three weeks and it has not been a success' (*DHS*, 190).

(The Canadian critic Magdalene Redekop remarks that the sisters' names hint at madness and Hell, just as the old maiden aunts represent the Fates, reminding readers of the anguish lying just below the narrative surface.)[15] The story is in two parts, both set in the present tense of Helen's visit, though in each part there are complex shifts back and forth in time as the story moves inexorably toward its final terrible revelation. Munro constructs a duplicitous world where everyday actuality is overlaid by memory and fictitious stories about the past, when at every turn the sisters confront their doubled selves as adults and as the adolescents they were ten years earlier. Ordinary sisterly rituals are an elaborate fabrication of good humour to disguise painful memories of their buried mother whose absent presence pervades her house like a restless ghost. This is really a Gothic plot about female imprisonment and betrayal; it deals with the uncanny as it hovers around the emblematic Gothic fear that what is dead and buried may not be dead at all but may come back to haunt the living. I have chosen this rather melo-dramatic scenario through which to read the central relation between two sisters and 'our Gothic Mother' as I wish to pay attention to Munro's first narrative representation of what Irigaray calls 'a highly explosive nucleus of emotions', that mother–daughter relationship which Munro refigures in different versions over thirty years.[16]

Helen, now a young mother herself, may have thought that by going to live in Vancouver she would be free of her family history, believing as she comes back to her mother's house for the first time in ten years that she faces 'the whole flatness and strangeness of the moment in which is revealed the source of legends, the unsatisfactory, apologetic and persistent reality' (DHS, 197). The house would seem to be empty: her mother is dead and her sister is at work, leaving only a jokey welcome note pinned on the door. However, as soon as she enters the house she is trapped in a haunted space, overpowered by once familiar rooms and objects. Her own carefully constructed adult identity starts to waver as she feels herself becoming all at once not only a mother and sister but also a daughter who stands in the hall instinctively waiting for the sound of her mother's 'ruined voice' calling out to her, and because that mother is now dead she can hear clearly what she had earlier refused to hear – a desperate cry for help. This reference to the absent mother's spectral voice is a traditional Gothic motif which goes back to the first female Gothics, with Ann Radcliffe's *A Sicilian Romance* (1792), and the peculiar power of this story seems to lie in its shifts between allusions to the Gothic literary tradition and the domestic horrors of real life. These fuse together in the account of a mother's degenerative illness which turns her into a prisoner trapped inside her own house where her dutiful daughters occupy double roles as nurses and prison guards. It is a story about monstrosity, love and betrayal told through the daughters' memories of their mother's helplessness and their own failures of love when faced with the impossible demands that her illness imposes on them. The key image in Helen's narrative is that of a photograph with multiple exposures:

> But I find the picture is still not complete. Our Gothic Mother, with the cold appalling mask of the Shaking Palsy laid across her features, shuffling, weeping, devouring attention wherever she can get it, eyes dead and burning, fixed inward on herself; this is not all. (*DHS*, 200)

Helen also remembers her mother's brief periods of recovery, her desperate struggle to live and her repeated failures to escape her illness. Her daughters too have failed to escape her illness, despite going away in turn to college and Helen's marriage; Maddy returned home to look after her mother and now Helen is back as well. They are still facing the problem of how to 'deal with Mother' even though she is dead, and all they can do is to tell stories about her, trying to distance themselves from the shame and embarrassment their mother's illness caused them. Like the sick mother's wanderings, the narrator's voice shifts restlessly between present and past, from adult recognition of the futility of their adolescent pain back into that earlier state:

> All wasted, our pride; our purging its rage in wild carica-
> tures we did for each other (no, not caricatures, for she was

one herself; imitations). We should have let the town have
her; it would have treated her better. (*DHS*, 195)

Though their mother became one of Jubilee's brief legends, for
the daughters to turn their mother into a legend is not so easy;
in death as in life she refuses to be silenced as her voice, her face,
and even her empty clothes come back to haunt them.

Why is the sick mother such a scandal to her daughters that
they wish to shut her up, to 'get rid of her' as the narrator puts
it in 'The Ottawa Valley', Munro's next unsuccessful attempt to
'deal with Mother'? Why do the daughters so cruelly deny her
the love and sympathy she craves? And how to assuage the guilt
and repair the damage in their own lives in the present? These
are the questions hovering over the story, and the answers
would seem to lie in a darker region of the psyche which is
intimately bound up with the dilemmas of female subjectivity
and a daughter's identity: 'My subjectivity is attached to the
presence of the other woman ... the woman-in-me is not silent,
she is part of a symbolic referential system.'[17] It is into this
referential system 'constituted by and of women themselves'
that Helen is forced to look in her traumatic visit to her two old
aunts in the second part of the story.

When Aunt Annie takes Helen upstairs to her 'neat and
virginal' bedroom, her revelations transform that place into 'the
black centre of the house with all other rooms leading to and
away from it.'[18] First she shows Helen her dead mother's clothes
and invites her to take some of them to wear, insisting on what
Irigaray has called the 'bodily encounter with the mother'.[19]
Although Helen can refuse to touch them she cannot refuse to
listen when her aunt tells of her mother's failed attempt to
escape from the hospital where Maddy had tricked her into
going for a check-up. It is an attempt at flight as desperate and as
doomed as that of the old mare Flora in 'Boys and Girls' another
story in this collection about female failure, but this is even
more threatening because it figures the enormity of the sisters'
betrayal which they have assiduously repressed:

Strangely, I felt no surprise, only a vague physical sense of terror, a longing not to be told – and beyond this a feeling that what I would be told I already knew, I had always known. (*DHS*, 207–8)

Again the mother refuses to stay buried, such is the transgressive power of old wives' tales, 'making sure the haunts we have contracted for are with us, not one gone without' (*DHS*, 209).

Perhaps Irigaray's comments on female hysteria may help to explain the daughters' fear of their 'Gothic Mother':

> There is a revolutionary potential in hysteria. Even in her paralysis, the hysteric exhibits a potential for gestures and desires … A movement of revolt and refusal, a desire for/ of the living mother … It is because they want neither to see nor hear that movement that they so despise the hysteric.[20]

All Helen's and Maddy's attempts to dismiss their mother end in failure. Back in the kitchen at home, there is no lightening of mood despite the afternoon sunlight, the children's noisy game, and the normal preparations for tea. Instead, there is a sudden eruption of suppressed emotion and the sound of shattering glass as Maddy 'loses her grip' and drops the bowl she is carrying. This is the time for the breaking open of secrets when Maddy confesses the intolerable strain of looking after her mother and her longing for a life of her own, while Helen speaking out of her own guilt urges her sister to go away as she had done. But no peace is made and the story ends with Maddy's desperate question, 'But why can't I, Helen? *Why can't I?*' (*DHS*, 210) That pink glass bowl now lying in fragments underlines the sense of irretrievable damage to a woman's life, told by a sister whose choice to leave home has made her an accomplice in their mother's death. This is the story of a failed exorcism ('No exorcising here' is repeated twice), a Gothic tale which figures primitive female fears – nothing less than fears of matricide – a 'more archaic murder' as Irigaray claims than Freud's theorising of the murder of the father.[21]

Munro reworks the sick mother story again and again, and her second version 'The Ottawa Valley' (written fifteen years later) rejects Gothic horror for a more realistic account of a twelve-year-old girl's response to the first intimations of her mother's illness.[22] The most unashamedly autobiographical of all Munro's stories, it traces the attempts of an adult daughter to construct a fitting memorial to her mother, though the compassionate remembering of her mother's life is continually played off against the child's pain and shock, and there is no elegiac sense of reconciliation at the end.

The story begins and ends in the present with the voice of the remembering narrator who is now the same age as her mother was when the first signs of Parkinson's Disease became visible:

> I think of my mother sometimes in department stores. I don't know why, I was never in one with her; their pleni-tude, their sober bustle, it seems to me, would have satisfied her. (*SIBM*, 218)

The plenitude and satisfaction which the daughter would like to offer in these opening sentences are then inexorably withdrawn in a story which denies the mother both. The daughter's memories are of her childhood visit to a poverty-stricken farm in the Ottawa Valley where her mother grew up, and of the multiple failures of her mother's modest social pretensions. There are many narrative strands that might be followed here,[23] though the one I wish to highlight is not so much the mother's life as the daughter's subjective remembering of her own loss. Why, when her Aunt Dodie announces that her mother has had 'a little stroke' (again, as in 'The Peace of Utrecht', the fatal taletelling of an aunt) is the daughter so afraid and angry? Why does she blame her mother for her 'helplessness'? And why does she see her mother as her betrayer, endlessly obsessed as she is with the moment of that mother's walking away from her and refusing her desperate demands for reassurance:

> But she did not do it. For the first time she held out altogether against me. She went on as if she had not heard, her familiar bulk ahead of me, turning strange, indifferent. She withdrew, she darkened in front of me, though all she did in fact was keep on walking along the path. (*SIBM*, 233)

Realism and slippage into unknown psychic territory sit side by side in these astonishing sentences, as the daughter remembers the traumatic experience of abandonment by her mother. As the most crucial moment in the story, it records a terrifying cluster of failure and loss – failure on the mother's part to live up to her all-powerful maternal image, loss of the daughter's infantile fantasy of that maternal omnipotence, and perhaps from the adult narrator's perspective, her later recognition of her own failure to allow her mother any independent life outside her maternal role. These perceptions, theorised by Irigaray as the refusal to let mothers be desiring subjects[24] and the loss of the myth of maternal plenitude, are here registered by Munro as the raw material of narrative.

The adult storytelling daughter still cannot stop her 'reckless pursuit' of her ever vanishing/dead mother, as the final meta-fictional commentary suggests. The mother's absent presence memorialised in the daughter's obsession with her physical body, her clothes, her shaking hands, her 'heaviness' refuses to be contained inside the frame of the 'proper story' in what is yet another failed exorcism. Like an incubus, she still 'weighs everything down'. While the other relatives in the Ottawa Valley may be remembered and their images stacked safely away like faded snapshots, her mother resists all the daughter's attempts to represent her for the edges of her image continue to 'melt and flow': 'She has stuck to me as close as ever and refused to fall away, and I could go on, and on, applying what skills I have, using what tricks I know, and it would always be the same' (*SIBM*, 235).[25]

Frequently Munro plays with the idea of the storyteller as trickster when she speculates on the powers and limits of storytelling, but nowhere does a storyteller's malice cause such disturbance as in 'Something I've Been Meaning to Tell You'. This story about two sisters, Et and Char, covers a period of forty years from a teenage romance in the summer of 1918 to late middle age and Char's death, possibly from a heart attack though possibly not. Composed of segments of narrative from the present and the past with gaps between them, the fragments are so arranged that connections may be made to reveal a shadowy pattern as the sisters' past repeats itself with variations. (This is a design that Munro uses frequently in her stories of the 1980s though it is quite unusual to see it in such a developed form in the early 1970s.) Behind the story of Et and Char lies another shadowy parallel out of the literary past coded in by allusions to the great medieval romance of King Arthur and Queen Guinevere, the tragic tale of a king's love and a queen's infidelity. As if to underline this connection, the narrating voice remarks when referring to Char's beauty, 'the qualities of legend were real … they surfaced where and when you least expected' (SIBM, 14). There are many stories in circulation here – local legends (which may or may not be true), echoes of Arthurian romance, a possible Gothic plot about jealousy and poisoning which looks very like an Agatha Christie detective story gone wrong – all contained within the story of two sisters who have lived in the small town of Mock Hill all their lives.[26]

The story would seem to be told from the point of view of the younger sister Et, but it is told in the third person (which may or may not be Et's voice) for Et is always the outsider, busily piecing together her narrative out of what she sees and what she wishes she could see, though there are always gaps in her story as well as possible distortions and certainly one crucial lie near the end. Introduced as gossip with its loosely digressive patterning, the story holds out the promise of revelation in its title, though that never comes. Instead we are told what we never expected to hear, a Gothic tale of a sister's jealousy and a modern version of tragic romance enacted in rural Ontario. The opening looks disarmingly conversational: 'Anyway he knows how to fascinate the women,' said Et to Char. She could not tell if Char went paler, hearing this, because Char was pale in the first place as anybody could get. She was like a ghost now, with her hair gone white. But still beautiful, she couldn't lose it' (SIBM, 9).

All the elements of the plot are here in this first paragraph: Et's malice, Char's ghostly beauty and the hints of a love story, but hidden behind a veil of ordinariness. The story proceeds in this oblique way by amplification and suggestion through Et's

account of her bus tour to see the local sites which include a
millionaire's mansion haunted by the ghost of a woman who
had poisoned her husband, 'a slow poison' as the guide informed
his passengers. Indeed it is the guide who fascinates Et, for
Blaikie Noble is a local lad who has now returned thirty years
later as a professional guide, visiting old haunts: 'Not visiting.
Haunting' (*SIBM*, 13). Et herself is haunted by the past,
especially by her memory of a single transgressive act, when as
a girl going outside late one night to get her dress from the
washing line, she had seen in the glimmering half light Blaikie
Noble and her sister Char making love under the lilac bush. She
catches a glimpse into the hidden territory of sexual desire
which lies closer to dreams then to waking life and she flees in
terror: 'Seeing their faces was enough for her' (*SIBM*, 18). But
of course it was not enough and this is the secret to which Et
returns again and again, trying to see more but never being able
to. Despite her sharp eyes she cannot see what she wishes to see,
so that inevitably her narrative proceeds by indirection: 'She
was never sure' (*SIBM*, 16) and 'Et had no way of knowing how
much of it was true.' (*SIBM*, 10). There are no clear distinctions
here between what is true and what Et has made up, but only
flashes of insight and clues which may or may not lead
anywhere. Obsessed by her sister and her secrets, Et becomes a
jealous watcher, cutting and fitting together fragments and clues
with all the professional skills she has learned as a dressmaker.
The story is full of secrets – not only Char's (Why did she try to
commit suicide when Blaikie Noble married somebody else?
Was Char trying to poison her devoted husband Arthur? Why
was there a bottle of rat poison in the kitchen cupboard?), but
also Et's secrets as well (Why did she hate her sister? Was she in
love with Arthur herself?). And why does Et tell Char after all
these years the lie that Blaikie Noble is going to marry a wealthy
woman who is visiting the hotel? 'She never knew where she got
the inspiration to say what she said, where it came from' (*SIBM*,
27). It seems to be an act of pure malice done 'to throw things
into confusion', which it certainly does, for Char dies of it. In
fact Et's lie is a simple repetition of an earlier incident when

Blaikie Noble had married a lady ventriloquist staying at the hotel and Char had tried to poison herself with washing blueing. The account of Char's death is left out of the narrative, so whether she drank the rat poison in the cupboard or died of a heart attack is something else that neither Et nor the reader will ever know. Blaikie Noble leaves town after the funeral, Arthur recovers and Et goes to live in his house to take care of him: 'If they had been married, people would have said they were very happy' (*SIBM*, 29).

This is the Arthur–Guinevere story told with an ironic ending: Guinevere's illicit romance with Sir Lancelot was revealed by Arthur's witch sister Morgan le Faye who was later killed by Lancelot, while Guinevere and Lancelot became penitents in religious houses. Not so in Ontario where the queen dies, Sir Lancelot departs, and Arthur lives on with the witch sister, though still adoring Char and keeping a picture of her dressed up as a statue in a play, on his bureau. Et carries her secret with her, for she is the bearer of the 'slow poison' of jealousy who is still planning to deal Arthur his death blow: 'She didn't believe she was going to let him die without knowing. He shouldn't be allowed' (*SIBM*, 29). This is not quite an Arthurian romance and not quite a Gothic tale, to which Munro might reply like one of her characters: 'It's not a story. It's something that happened' (*MJ*, 215).

'Dance of the Happy Shades' is a story which came to Munro from 'outside' in the form of 'an anecdote told at a family dinner-party'[27] about an old music teacher's annual piano recital in Toronto, yet in the telling Munro reimagines it from the 'inside' with her characteristic transformations of ordinariness. There is another sense in which this story comes from 'outside' as well, for it has distinct affinities with Eudora Welty's story 'June Recital' in *The Golden Apples* about another old music teacher in the small town of Morgana, Mississippi.[28] 'June Recital' tells the story of a fantastic attempt by an old mad German music teacher called Miss Eckhart to recreate the scene of one of her recitals in a derelict house on the main street in Morgana, which she then tries to burn down like a funeral pyre.

Her attempt fails however and she is taken off to the lunatic asylum. In Welty's story domestic space is transformed into a theatre of tragic farce and humiliation, for Miss Eckhart is the figure of a failed woman artist, excessive, passionate and foreign, who lived for her music and tried to lavish her gifts on her pupils, opening up worlds of the imagination dangerously beyond Morgana, which nobody had wanted. Central to the story is a remembered Beethoven *Fantasia* played at one recital by a girl called Virgie Rainey with such passion that the red dye of her sash bleeds over her white dress as if she had been stabbed to the heart – an image of the sacrifice to art which this girl later betrays.

It is almost as if to redeem this image of the failure and frustration of the woman artist that Munro writes her revision of 'June Recital'. In 'Dance of the Happy Shades' old Miss Marsalles (at what is surely her last music recital) is quite as grotesque a figure as Miss Eckhart in her long brocaded dress, looking like 'a character in a masquerade' or 'the feverish, fancied-up courtesan of an unpleasant Puritan imagination' (*DHS*, 217); the setting is just as incongruous where a tumbledown house in Morgana is shadowed by a hot little house in downtown Toronto with flies crawling over the party food; the atmosphere is just as disconcerting: 'There is a feeling that can hardly be put into words about Miss Marsalles' parties; things are getting out of hand, anything may happen' (*DHS*, 212). Here too music is the disturbing foreign language, the message from elsewhere, as Gluck's 'Danse des ombres heureuses' is played at the recital by a Down's syndrome pupil called Dolores Boyle. 'The mothers sit, caught with a look of protest on their faces ... as if reminded of something they had forgotten they had forgotten' (*DHS*, 222), being forced out of politeness to sit and listen to the wonderful music. The only person who is unsurprised is old Miss Marsalles for as Munro says, 'people who believe in miracles do not make much fuss when they actually encounter one' (*DHS*, 223). However, in Toronto as in Morgana such an exceptional per-formance is unexpected and unacceptable; it is either a 'trick' or a 'miracle' depending on the listener's point of view. It does not fit on the social map any more than Virgie Rainey's playing had done, and the mothers are glad to go home, leaving 'Miss Marsalles and her no longer possible parties behind, quite certainly forever' (*DHS*, 224). Yet in Munro's story Miss Marsalles is not defeated like Miss Eckhart; on the contrary she is vindicated, for the music becomes a sign of redemption, 'that one communiqué from the other country where she lives' (*DHS*, 224), as it opens out into the unmapped spaces of art and the imagination.

This is a more optimistic ending than Welty's, though I believe that Munro learned a great deal from Welty's stories about ways of translating the multidimensional social map of small-town life into fiction. There is a similarly fine double awareness of community values and also of what goes on outside or within or alongside daily life, just as there is a strong affinity between them in the way they use maps and houses in their storytelling to describe the different ways a place is known to the different people living in it, be it Ontario or Mississippi. Both Munro and Welty leave us with the sense of a familiar place which is also full of secret alternative spaces; they both offer a very feminine kind of mapping where the perception of difference emerges from inside the grid of social and symbolic order. Such textual mapping is neither revolutionary nor confrontational, but it is profoundly disruptive in its challenge to traditional structures of authority as it points obliquely towards that 'other country' which is the space of what Irigaray calls 'the feminine imaginary'.[29]

Secrets and discoveries:
Lives of Girls and Women

> So lying alongside our world was Uncle Benny's world like
> a troubling distorted reflection, the same but never at all
> the same.[1]

LIVES of Girls and Women is the story of a girl called Del Jordan
living in Jubilee, Ontario who grows up to become a writer, and
I begin this discussion with Del's childish discovery of how
different her own world can look when viewed from somebody
else's perspective, almost as if there are alternative worlds which
challenge each other as different representations of reality.
Recorded near the beginning of the book, this discovery of Del's is
emblematic of the 'double vision' which is so characteristic of
Munro's fiction. There is 'our world,' the solid familiar world
which Del knows in her parents' house, and there is also Uncle
Benny's world where ordinariness seems to be refracted through
a distorting mirror, yet both seem to be representations of the
same place. Like overlapping maps of the same territory, their
doubleness undermines any singular interpretation of place or
event. Told from Del's point of view, the stories make connections between different perceptions of reality, slipping from
everyday ordinariness into imagined worlds and the hidden
topography of fantasy. Though Munro is not a fantasy writer her
stories expose the limits of realism by working within a
referential framework and then collapsing it by shifting into a
different fictional mode. Her narrative method provokes the
question which she asks in a different context, 'What is real'?[2]
As Munro shows, fantasy works with the same materials as

realistic fiction but it arranges them according to different imperatives, not of rationality or social convention but of fear and desire, revealing another side to the story or (to shift metaphors) laying out an alternative secret geography which exists in the same place. Both realism and fantasy are revealed as narrative conventions for translating reality into words though they work according to different principles, each leaving out a dimension which the other includes and each disrupting the other's design.[3] In Del's storytelling method (which is also Munro's) both kinds of discourse are present. Indeed they are interchangeable, so that the familiar and the unfamiliar are both contained within the same narrative structure. In *Lives of Girls and Women* as the title promises, everything is in the plural for the stories enclose disparate and often contradictory views within the same fictional space, 'the same but never at all the same'.

It may seem strange to emphasise plurality when this is one woman's narrative about her childhood and adolescence up to the point when she fails to get her university scholarship but decides to leave her home town anyway. Yet double vision is implicit within the form of fictive autobiography as the story is told by an older Del who reveals that she has become the writer she desired to be in the 'Epilogue' to this book. Similarly, any attempt to map the development of female subjectivity will be characterised by multiplicity as a girl like Del endlessly invents and reinvents personae for herself, some of them idealised and imaginary, some of them created in resistance to the role models offered by her mother and the women in her family and social community. Del's 'self' is constructed very like a text as it offers a variety of images, a tangle of signifiers, made up through stories whose meanings are continually unsettled by the next episode, for Del is in process of forging her identity as a woman and an artist. Many critics have pointed out that *Lives* is a feminised version of James Joyce's *A Portrait of the Artist as a Young Man*, while the feminist critic Barbara Godard has spelled out some of the differences that gender makes here.[4] Del may be the heroine of her own life story but she is implicated in the female condition, and Munro shows how writing about one girl's life involves writing about many other women's lives. Del is both different from her mother, her aunts and her girlfriends and yet also like them, a product of Jubilee and its small town value system in the 1940s and 1950s.

LGW is the only one of Munro's fictions to be published as a 'novel', though in an interview she suggests a refinement of that classification by describing it as an 'episodic novel'.[5] It might be described as a novel with built-in fragmentation, where Del tells many people's stories as well as her own and offers many alternative ways of mapping the life of her home town. It is a *Bildungsroman* with a decentralised narrative structure, and I prefer the classification offered by A. J. Gurr who recognises both the multiplicity of voices and perspectives in *Lives* and also the continuity of focus through a single narrator by describing it as a 'whole book story sequence' comparable with Joyce's *Dubliners* and constituting a distinctive genre in contemporary Canadian writing.[6] I shall refer to the sections not as chapters (they have never been numbered as such) but by their individual titles. We know that Munro began with the intention of producing a conventional novel but gradually came to realise that the medium of separate but interlinked stories was more suited to her talents. She described the stages of her writing process and the resulting structure of *LGW* when she told J. R. (Tim) Struthers how she began with a story about Del's mother called 'Princess Ida':

> Then I saw it was going to work into a novel, and then I went on and on writing what I thought was a novel. Then I saw it wasn't working. So I went back and picked out of that novel 'Princess Ida' in its original form – I had changed it to make it into the novel – and I picked out 'Age of Faith', 'Changes and Ceremonies', and 'Lives of Girls and Women'. Then, having written all those separate sections, I wrote 'Baptizing'. Then I went back and wrote the first two sections, the one about Uncle Benny, 'The Flats Road' … and 'Heirs of the Living Body.' And then I wrote the 'Epilogue: The Photographer' which gave me *all* kinds of trouble.[7]

Such scrupulously detailed remembering is indicative not only of Munro's methods of composition but also of the finished stories themselves. Their characteristic development is not linear but oblique and digressive, like a process of discovering secrets in unsuspected places: 'Mostly in my stories I like to look at what people don't understand. What we don't understand. What we think is happening and what we understand later on.'[8] W. R. Martin has suggested that the stories in *LGW* are like 'pictures hanging together', offering multiple images but never a unified whole, taking his description from 'Changes and Ceremonies': 'Though there is no plausible way of hanging those pictures together – if the last one [of the schoolteacher Miss Farris floating face down, drowned in the Wawanash River] is true, then must it not alter the others? – they are going to have to stay together now' (*LGW*, 139).[9] Things may not fit together, yet somehow they must remain together as those disparate elements of life which all have to be accommodated within Del's account.

The stories through which Del maps her life are related to the traditional subjects of women's writing and of Canadian small-town fiction, and I shall focus my discussion on four in particular, which demonstrate both Del's distinctive sensibility and some wider social issues, 'all these realities' as Munro calls them.[10] 'The Flats Road' provides a map of the whole territory of *LGW* with its representation of southwestern Ontario landscape and its multiple geographies, perceived through Del's double vision as she moves between real and imagined worlds. In this opening story told from a child's perspective (but with flashes of an adult narrator's retrospective insight) my main concern will be with location and representations of landscape.[11] My analysis will include both a structuralist reading of landscape and to some extent a deconstruction of that design, showing how realism is transformed within the text.

To some extent I shall use the same methods of analysis in the other stories, demonstrating significant stages in Del's growing up process as she questions conventional frames of reference in order to record other ways of reading reality. 'Heirs of the Living Body' is concerned with uncovering buried maps of the past through writing local history and the history of her own family, who have been in the same area since its settlement in the late 1860s and 1870s. This story raises wider issues of how to write about Canadian pioneer history which Munro continues to explore in her later collections through stories like 'Chaddeleys and Flemings' (*MJ*), 'Meneseteung' (*FMY*) and 'A Wilderness Station' (*OS*). There is also the question of young Del's position as inheritor of a body of family traditions through which Munro figures a woman's ambivalent relation to her cultural and literary inheritance. 'Baptizing' is arguably the most important story in *LGW* for it focuses on crucial moments in Del's adolescent quest to define her self. It deals with a significant stage in Del's education, where in her last year at high school she falls in love and has her first real sexual experience (though she refuses to be baptised). The story outlines Del's growing awareness of the complex social geography of Jubilee, especially places out of bounds like the Gay-la Dance Hall 'half a mile north of town, on the highway' (which her mother refers to as 'Sodom and Gomorrah') and the wilderness territory down beside the Wawanash River where Del goes with her lover Garnet French, crossing over into an eroticised landscape of sexual desire. Del is nearly drowned in the river, like at least two other female casualties in Jubilee, Miss Farris and Marion Sherriff. However hers is not suicide but a desperate struggle for independence and she manages to escape, trudging back home on her own: 'As I walked on into Jubilee I repossessed the world' (*LGW*, 236–7).

It is only in the final story 'Epilogue: The Photographer' that Del's narrative is transformed into the story of a writer's life. As Munro told Struthers: 'Up until now this was not the story of the artist as a young girl. It was just the story of a young girl. And this introduced a whole new element, which I felt had not been sufficiently prepared for. And yet, I found eventually that the book didn't mean anything to me without it.'[12] As readers we see only the final version and as usual, endings condition our perspective on what has gone before. This last story which deals with Del's failed attempt to write a Gothic novel about Jubilee offers a metafictional comment on the relation between realism and fantasy. It also draws a suggestive parallel between novelist and photographer, focusing on problems of representation through the media of photography and story-telling. Such problems would also apply to history, mapping and painting, which like all forms of artifice do not mirror reality but instead offer interpretations of it. As Roland Barthes asked in his famous essay on the *Blue Guide*, how does one justly represent a place or the lives of the people in that place when any representation risks suppressing 'the reality of the land and that of its people?'[13] Del rephrases the same problem, 'It is a shock, when you have dealt so cunningly, powerfully, with reality, to come back and find it still there' (*LGW*, 247). The challenge of an untranslatable reality is the challenge which she constantly faces and tries to resolve by different storytelling methods, always knowing that 'people's lives, in Jubilee as elsewhere, were dull, simple, amazing, and unfathomable – deep caves paved with kitchen linoleum (*LGW*, 249).

A structuralist approach to landscape in 'The Flats Road' would focus on binary oppositions such as surfaces and depths, the exteriors and interiors of houses, Jubilee town centre and the surrounding countryside, while a deconstructive reading would pay more attention to areas hidden within the town map or unscripted spaces like the deep holes in the Wawanash River, whose very existence suggest alternative less municipally authorised ways of mapping the same territory. The story begins not in town or at home but down by the banks of the river where Del and her young brother Owen are splashing about in the mud catching frogs for their father's hired man Uncle Benny: 'He was not our uncle, nor anybody's' (*LGW*, 2). They are deep in the landscape under the willows with their legs being cut by blades of sword grass. There is a pervasive sense of being on the edges of the unknown which is increased as the children follow the track across the fields to Uncle Benny's shabby unpainted house on the edge of the bush with caged wild animals in the yard. Uncle Benny is himself an eccentric marginalised figure though it is his house which fascinates Del. That house is pure Ontario Gothic: shabby and unpainted on the outside, it is like an enormous junkheap, 'a whole rich, dark, rotting mess' of other people's rubbish – worn-out furniture, chipped dishes, broken toasters – not to mention the scandalous newspapers which Del sits there avidly reading on the sagging porch because she knows better than to take any of them home. These papers do not have news about the war (though this is the early 1940s); instead they are full of reports of sensational crimes:

'FATHER FEEDS TWIN DAUGHTERS TO HOGS/ WOMAN GIVES BIRTH TO HUMAN MONKEY/ VIRGIN RAPED ON CROSS BY CRAZED MONKS/ SENDS HUSBAND'S TORSO BY MAIL (*LGW*, 5).

This is the peculiar news from Uncle Benny's surreal world for he inhabits a dimension entirely different from the every-day, as Del realises walking home across the fields: 'The nearer I got to home the more this vision faded' and the more unlikely it seemed 'that a woman would really send her husband's torso, wrapped in Christmas paper, by mail to his girl friend in South Carolina' (*LGW*, 5). The very sight of the plain back walls of her house casts doubt on the existence of that other world whose mysterious messages so thrilled and horrified Del.

Yet Del's house 'at the end of the Flats Road' which is the centre of her world is itself on the margins of Jubilee's urban world with its 'sidewalks, street lights, lined-up shade trees, milk-men's and icemen's carts, birdbaths, flower borders, verandas with wicker chairs' (*LGW*, 5–6). All these amenities are lacking on the Flats Road with its neglected houses and its odd social mix of bootleggers, retired prostitutes, cripples, idiots, and Del's parents who run a struggling silver fox farm. This is borderline territory which is 'not part of town but it was not part of the country either' (*LGW*, 6). Del herself crosses between these different worlds with ease and as a child of seven she has no problems with location when she is writing out Uncle Benny's address in full on a letter: '*Mr Benjamin Thomas Poole, The Flats Road, Jubilee, Wawanash County, Ontario, Canada,*

North America, The Western Hemisphere, The World, The Solar System, The Universe' (*LGW*, 11). Needless to say Uncle Benny suggests an alternative geography, 'Where is that in relation to Heaven?'

Uncle Benny's house is the scenario for his failed marriage which is as grotesque as any Gothic plot, for it contains a mad-woman and hidden domestic violence which Del is forbidden to see. In answer to a newspaper advertisement Uncle Benny acquires a bride called Madeleine Howey and her illegitimate small daughter Diane. Madeleine herself is rather like Uncle Benny's wild animals or Del's father's silver foxes, unstable and occasionally violent, 'a borderline case' according to Del's mother, and one day Uncle Benny returns home to find that she has left, taking away her daughter and some of his precious things. Only then does it emerge (or appear to emerge, for it is Del's mother's interpretation) that she has been beating Diane. Uncle Benny sets off to drive to Toronto to find the child and bring her back. Of course he does not find her and gets hopelessly lost in the big city, for he travels without a road map. Yet when he returns, the story he tells about his travels offers an alternative map of Toronto, for 'a map of the journey was burnt into his mind'. Instead of urban streets and sidewalks, his Toronto landscape is a sinister wasteland, another kind of rubbish heap where objects lose their conventional meanings:

> And as he talked a different landscape – cars, billboards, industrial buildings, roads and locked gates and high wire fences, railway tracks, steep cindery embankments, tin sheds, ditches with a little brown water in them, also tin cans, mashed cardboard cartons, all kinds of clogged or barely floating waste – all this seemed to grow up around us ... It was his triumph, that he couldn't know about, to make us see. (*LGW*, 25–6)

It is also Munro's triumph to make her readers see that other world alongside the everyday, offering a glimpse into some of the multiple worlds hidden inside conventional maps of place.

The story ends with Del's image of her own family's domestic space which reassuringly protects her from the 'howling weather outside', though she knows that it is still there. As for the vanished Madeleine, she is soon relegated to the status of local legend: 'Madeleine! That madwoman!' (*LGW*, 26). The ending illustrates the process by which social order is maintained, as it centres on the familiar and excludes the odd, rather like closing the door of a house on the outside world. The child's sense of security returns though the memory of Madeleine 'going down the road in her red jacket with her legs like scissors, flinging abuse over her shoulder' remains. By paying attention to maps and to the hidden spaces within them, Del's narrative weaves together signs which produce a plurality of meanings in the landscape of Jubilee and beyond it, as far as the 'bush' on one side and Toronto on the other.

'Heirs of the Living Body' is a story about another of Del's uncles (a real one this time), her great-uncle Craig, and his death and funeral when she is around twelve-years old. His dead body at the centre of the narrative poses questions about Del's relation to the 'living body' of her family together with the wider question of how to record the 'living body' of history from a woman's point of view. The custodian of tradition is the patriarchal figure of Uncle Craig, clerk of Fairmile township, chronicler of the history of Wawanash County since its settlement in the 1860s and keeper of the family tree 'going back to 1670, in Ireland'. His typewritten historical account focuses on what *men* have done, for men's work is public and worthy to be recorded (even if, like the men in Del's family, they have done 'nothing remarkable') while women's work is private and domestic, and therefore not worthy. Uncle Craig provides historical documentation, constructing 'a solid, intricate structure of lives supporting us from the past', an image as reassuring as his own solid brick house. However, even as a child Del challenges his representation by drawing attention to what he leaves out, preferring an imaginative retrieval of the secret histories of unmarked places which have been lost behind official accounts. Such evidence is available, like the photograph on Uncle Craig's office wall of the original log cabin built on that wilderness site: 'That picture seemed to have been in another country, where everything was much lower, muddier, darker than here' (*LGW*, 28). However, Uncle Craig chooses to ignore it.

Approaching history from a different angle, Del manages to tell her version as a revelation of the lives of some of the girls and women within this social structure – Aunt Elspeth and Auntie Grace who are Uncle Craig's sisters and who keep house for him, Aunt Moira and her handicapped daughter Mary Agnes, and Del's own mother who inhabits yet another world, that of the 1950s woman struggling towards an economic and intellectual independence, a precursor of the feminism to come. Every one of these women's lives is different from the others, so that the living body of family history begins to look less like a solid structure and more like a mosaic of secret worlds coexisting under the surface of ordinariness. As the inheritor of all these 'living bodies' Del tries to make up the story of her own life:

> I … exchanged my mother's world of serious skeptical questions, endless but somehow disregarded housework, lumps in the mashed potatoes, and unsettling ideas, for theirs of work and gaiety, comfort and order, intricate formality. There was a whole new language to learn in their house. (*LGW*, 37)

It is however Mary Agnes, 'deprived of oxygen in the birth canal,' who terrifies Del, not by the stories she tells but by the secrets she keeps. Through her Del is forced to confront the mystery of death – first the dead cow and later the dead body of Uncle Craig. In Mary Agnes's company Del really looks for the first time at a cow, seeing the markings on its hide like a 'gleaming strange map of another country', but the map is obscured by Mary Agnes's hand held in front of Del's face, so that it exists as an emblem of the mystery surrounding her in her everyday life. As Aritha van Herk remarks in her essay on cartography in Canadian fiction, 'Men map the territory of place, history and event [while] the female fiction writers of Canada map a different territory, not as obvious but just as important. They map the country of the interior, the world maze of the human being.'[14]

Del uses that image of the maze to describe Uncle Craig's house after his death. A safe place has been transformed into an intricate puzzle with a 'black dot' at its centre, the dot being Uncle Craig's coffin which is to be avoided at all costs and yet cannot be avoided. Del perceives that the mystery of death is an excess term which cannot be accommodated on any map, though its presence is felt 'floating around loose, ignored but powerful' (*LGW*, 46). It is the great disrupter of continuity, whatever her mother might say in her advanced speculative way about the beauty of organ transplants and the transcendence of death. At the funeral Del tries to retreat from the rituals of death by going out into the old store-room at the back of the house which is filled with objects from the past; but even there she cannot escape being a member of the living body, as Mary Agnes reminds her. Indeed Del cannot even bite her way out of the family though she sinks her teeth into Mary Agnes's arm, for 'freedom is not so easily come by'; Del is forgiven and restored with tea and cake. Later as a teenager, still crossing between home and her aunts' house which has become 'like a tiny sealed-off country', Del even has to accept the gift of her uncle's unfinished county history. Though she discards the manuscript as 'dead, heavy and useless' and lets it rot in the basement, using the large black tin box for her own poems and bits of an unfinished novel, yet much later she herself becomes a teller of local history. Del discovers that she is her uncle's true heir, though with a difference, for she presents another possibility for women not even envisaged by Uncle Craig but entrusted to her by her aunts. Committed like him to 'getting everything in and still making it read smooth' (*LGW*, 61), Del insists on telling the story in her own way. As a female chronicler she writes in the women's stories which her uncle has omitted, while as a novelist she shows how traditional realistic writing can be made to include moments of intense subjectivity and visionary perception, illuminating some of the dark secrets hidden within the living body of history. Del's re-visionary enterprise suggests one answer to the Canadian critic Barbara Godard's questions about female authorship: 'How does one write as a woman? Does one write like the fathers ... or does one 'write' like the mothers in the separate tradition of oral literature, creating with the body, on the margins?'[15]

'Baptizing', with its suggestions of initiation ceremonies, signals crucial stages in Del's experience on the threshold of adulthood. It might be described as a journey of discovery, for it is concerned with choices and consequences and with Del's recognition of her own difference from other young men and women in Jubilee. Our topic of inquiry might be described as mapping female subjectivity within Canadian landscape. The spaces to be mapped are multiple for they extend beyond topography to include the social geographies of Jubilee as well as the fantasy territory of Del's imagination. As the longest story in the collection (almost novella length with its 64 pages), 'Baptizing' is structured like a quest in six narrative sections with breaks between them. Though Del achieves some sense of her distinctive identity, this is not to suggest that any point of closure is reached. It never is, for Munro's stories undermine the notion of a single identity by showing that the selves of her protagonists are far less stable than the word 'identity' suggests. The narrative structure emphasises discontinuity, crisis and indeterminacy as it traces Del's changing relationships and the choices she makes.

The story begins with the break-up of established patterns in school life and friendships as her old friend Naomi moves away from academic subjects into the 'cool ordinary light' of business studies and then quickly out of school into a new social sphere as a working girl. Gone are the days when she and Del giggled about love and sex, 'laughing ourselves sick about it' (*LGW*, 181) or scrawled obscenities in lipstick on the mirrors in the ladies' toilet at the Town Hall. As Naomi changes into a well-groomed office girl, adopting all the conventional aspirations of 1950s femininity where marriage and homemaking are a girl's only legitimate ambitions, Del finds herself adopting an attitude of vigorous resistance to that reductive feminine mystique as it is proposed in songs, fashions and popular psychology articles in the magazines Del reads: 'I wanted men to love me *and* I wanted to think of the universe when I looked at the moon' (*LGW*, 178). Del's exploration of the possibilities for women's lives extends beyond Naomi's small-town horizons into legendary scenarios as she listens by herself on Saturday afternoons to the Metropolitan Opera radio broadcasts, slipping sideways into the imaginary spaces created by the music of *Lucia di Lammermoor*, *Carmen* and *La Traviata* with their throbbing moments of passion and glorious self transformations. Nourished on such images of female heroism, Del cannot be satisfied with the mundane teenage pleasures of getting drunk at the Gay-la Dance Hall or joking around in a bedroom at the Brunswick Hotel with Naomi and her boyfriends. Even though she is drunk for the first time in her life, Del's unconscious resistance causes her to walk away from that room, climb down the fire escape and then totter home alone: 'Putting my shoes on, I was bewildered; I had really meant to go back to the room' (*LGW*, 189). With Del preferring to read Elizabeth Gaskell's *Life of Charlotte Brontë* rather than to follow Naomi's path, their long school friendship comes to an end: 'I felt she had moved as far beyond me, in what I vaguely and worriedly supposed to be the real world, as I in all sorts of remote and useless and special knowledge, taught in schools, had moved beyond her' (*LGW*, 192).

By contrast, the second section focuses on Del's friendship with a boy in the last year of high school, as it explores sexist stereotypes and Del's search to find a voice for her imaginative intelligence. (Her role will ultimately be that of female novelist, though she does not know it yet.) Just as she resists Naomi's definitions of feminine destiny as inadequate, so she also resists her mother's feminist aspirations as too asexual and intellectual. She is the brightest girl in her class ('I got A's at school. I never had enough of them,' *LGW*, 192) and her closest friendship is with the cleverest boy, Jerry Storey (whose 'IQ puts him in the top *quarter* of the top one percent of the population' as his mother proudly informs her). Munro uses their cheerfully competitive relationship to explore issues of gendered expectations in relation to intelligence. Grouped together as 'The Brains Trust', they both wish for academic glory: 'what really drew and kept us together were these hopes, both denied and admitted, both ridiculed and respected in each other' (*LGW*, 196). Yet there the similarities end, for Jerry is the typical brainy boy with a passion for science and an intellectual arrogance which automatically assumes that Del as a girl would have 'almost no capacity for abstract thought' (*LGW*, 193). What he does not realise in his thoughtless adoption of sexist stereotypes is that his male ego is being protected by Del's feminine sensibility – though the image Del uses here offers an astute critique of the power of the phallus: 'I felt in him what women feel in men, something so tender, swollen, tyrannical, absurd; I would never take the consequences of interfering with it: I had an indifference, a contempt almost, that I concealed from him' (*LGW*, 193–4).

Despite the sexual connotations of this image, their friendship is not based on sex at all but rather on its opposite, as the two of them deliberately parody teenage dating habits and take a mocking delight in the grotesqueries of the body. Indeed their one attempt at sex ends in fiasco when Jerry's mother comes home early and he in fright pushes Del naked into the cellar, sending her clothes down the laundry shoot after her. Del makes another of her escapes – this time through the cellar window – then runs home barelegged through the snow. The transformation of this absurd event into a 'Great Comic Scene, something jerky and insane from a silent movie' (*LGW*, 203) marks their shared awareness that there were other more important things than sex to think about, like the scholarship exams where they both wanted 'glory, glory, the top of the pinnacled A's, security at last' (*LGW*, 204).

However, the third and subsequent sections of this story record a radical disruption in the rhythms of Del's life when she falls in love with a boy called Garnet French whom she meets at a religious revival meeting at the Town Hall and embarks on a passionate affair with him at the very time of studying for the scholarship exams. As I have written about Munro's treatment of female romantic fantasy in my first chapter and about this episode elsewhere[16] I shall focus here on Del's youthful discourse of desire and sexual discovery. The girl who was on a quest for academic success now finds herself caught in the scenarios of novels and operas where her lover represents the 'intrusion of the legendary into the real world' (*LGW*, 211). Though the blossoming of this teenage romance comes as a sudden surprise to Del, the reader is probably not surprised, for there is a curious signal at the end of the previous section which alerts us: 'My need for love had gone underground, like a canny toothache' (*LGW*, 205). That word 'canny' together with the references to the hidden life of the unconscious encourages us to see Del's romance with Garnet as a return of the repressed. 'Canny'/'uncanny', the 'Unheimlich' as the uncovering 'of all that needs to remain hidden if the world is to be comfortably known'[17] are the terms which best describe such revelations of concealed desire. The whole episode shimmers with fantasy from the moment when Garnet comes to stand beside her during the hymn-singing at the revival meeting. 'Revival' is an ironic term in this context, or perhaps it merely points to similar urges for self transcendence between the religious and the erotic: 'I felt angelic with gratitude, truly as if I had come out on another level of existence' (*LGW*, 210).

For Del, falling in love is a process of discovery which opens up hitherto unknown territory, where lovemaking down in the wilderness beside the Wawanash River allows Del and Garnet to 'cross over, going into a country where there was perfect security' (*LGW*, 228). Yet the fantastic is always mapped in relation to the real world, and Del is consistently aware of herself as inhabiting borderline territory: 'I had that strange and confident sensation of being in a dream from which I would presently wake up' (*LGW*, 213). Though she aspires to those epiphanic moments of self-surrender and transformation promised by romantic fantasy, what she discovers is quite different. When she experiences her first orgasm it does nothing to obliterate her sense of self but rather enhances it: 'I was amazed to undergo it in company, so to speak; it did seem almost too private, even lonely a thing, to find at the heart of love' (*LGW*, 226). She finds herself in the position of the dreamer who is also outside her own dream, with all 'my differences, my reservations, my life' (*LGW*, 235). She is as isolated as she has ever been, and the crisis comes when Garnet directly challenges Del's fantasy by asking her to marry him. She realises that she does not want a husband; she wants a romantic lover: 'I meant to keep him sewed up in his golden lover's skin forever' (*LGW*, 234). When romance threatens to turn into a trap Del resists it at the peril of her life as Garnet's playful attempt to baptise her in the river becomes an attempt to subdue her by drowning her. Once again she escapes and then walks home alone, back into Jubilee where the map is reassuringly still in place: 'As I walked on into Jubilee I repossessed the world. Trees, houses, fences, streets, came back to me, in their own sober and familiar shapes ... And already I felt my old self – my old devious, ironic, isolated self – beginning to breathe again and stretch and settle' (*LGW*, 236–7).

Far from finishing off everything she was before, Del's love affair has confirmed her sense of isolated selfhood, while giving her some insight into the delicious rhythms of her own body and of the painful contradictions between fantasy and reality. At the end Del sits alone in her mother's house; she has failed to win her scholarship but she has fought free of the choices offered by Naomi, Jerry, Garnet, and of her mother's academic ambitions for her. Returning to the printed word, not in schoolbooks this time but in newspaper advertisements for jobs in the city, Del decides to escape from Jubilee and she chooses yet another persona for herself 'getting on a bus, like girls in movies leaving home, convents, lovers' (*LGW*, 238). What Del has learned is that the achievement of independence is not so simple as fictions of masculinity would have her believe: 'Men were supposed to be able to go out and take on all kinds of experiences and shuck off what they didn't want and come back proud' (*LGW*, 174). The reality of Del's feminine experience is very different, as the final sentence echoes her own vivid sense of self division:

> *Garnet French, Garnet French, Garnet French.*
> *Real Life.* (*LGW*, 238)

'Epilogue: The Photographer' caused Munro a great deal of trouble ('I was about half as long again writing that as writing the whole book').[18] Coming at the end, it casts a retrospective glance back over the whole book and glances forward into the future, giving a wider perspective on Del's narrative, for this is the story where a 'girl's life' becomes a 'writer's life'. What is the connection between writing and photography? Why does the story begin with a reference to death ('This town is rife with suicides', *LGW*, 239)? And why in this evidently self-reflexive account does Del compare her activity of writing with photography and not with painting or cartography? The answers would seem to lie in the kind of fiction Del has chosen to write and in her anxiety over the problem of representation. Though the older Del may choose to write within a dominantly realistic genre, she remembers that when she was young she preferred Gothic novels like *Wuthering Heights* with their dark secrets and melodramatic violence, and it is the young Del who writes the black fable here about the Photographer. Photography, as Roland Barthes points out so brilliantly in his *Camera Lucida*, is the art which is closest to realistic recording as the photograph is 'always *something* which is represented'.[19] Yet paradoxically in catching likeness to life the photograph is also death-dealing; Barthes speaks of its 'embalming' power while he also suggests that photographers, 'determined upon the capture of actuality, do not know that they are agents of Death'.[20] Del would seem to be an exception here for she does know that the Photographer deals in death, and though she does not understand the implications of her Gothic tale, she uses the mask of the Photographer to figure everything that she fears about the duplicities of a writer's profession with its possible distortions and betrayals of reality.

Del begins her account by glancing back to a time before her last summer in Jubilee awaiting the scholarship exam results, to that moment when she decided to become a writer: 'I saw that the only thing to do with my life was to write a novel' (*LGW*, 240). It was, as she later sees, another kind of fantasy like her Carmen persona or her love affair with Garnet French, a glamourising transformation of Jubilee into 'an older, darker, more decaying town' which obscures the real place for her, and she compares her unwritten Gothic novel to a magic box in a fairy story: 'I just kept hold of the idea of the novel, and felt better' (*LGW*, 241). Del's central characters are based on the Sherriff family in Jubilee, one of whose members, old Mrs Sherriff, had fascinated Del as a child when she went illicitly to the Anglican church (*LGW*, 91–114). One of the Sherriff sons is an alcoholic, another spends frequent periods in the local asylum and the daughter Marion was one of the famous town suicides who drowned herself in the Wawanash River. Del's Gothic heroine Caroline ('blotting out altogether the pudgy Marion') becomes pregnant by the sinister travelling Photographer and she too drowns herself in the Wawanash River. As Del remarks, 'That was all. Except …'. Of course it is not all, for the fascinating figure here is the Photographer or rather his photographs:

> The pictures he took turned out to be unusual, even frightening. People saw that in his pictures they had aged twenty or thirty years. Middle-aged people saw in their own features the terrible, growing, inescapable likeness of their dead parents … Brides looked pregnant, children adenoidal. So he was not a popular photographer, though cheap.(*LGW*, 242–3)

The oddity of these pictures is that they photograph the passage of time, revealing what is unseen on the surface but 'what is nonetheless already there'. That phrase is taken from Barthes's description of the 'punctum' in a photograph, which is the crucial additional detail which transforms a photographic image from realistic record into a *representation* of reality. Interestingly, it is just such a process which Del describes in making her Gothic fiction about Jubilee as she challenges conventional maps in an attempt to reveal hitherto invisible secret landscapes: 'The main thing was that it seemed true to me, not real but true, as if I had discovered, not made up, such people and such a story, as if that town was lying close behind the one I walked through every day' (*LGW*, 244).

Barthes also remarks on the 'insidiousness' of photographs, which 'sometimes make appear what we never see in a real face: a genetic feature, fragment of oneself or of a relative which comes from some ancestor'.[21] A point of connection may therefore be established between the Gothic photographs in Del's novel and her act of writing fiction, where she reveals her lineage as Uncle Craig's inheritor. The disreputable Photographer with his lank black hair and pasty skin is a malignant transformer of reality, and indeed this is the point of comparison with Del as she initially sees her role as novelist. Walking home one evening with Jerry Storey, she is able to see Jubilee in all its ordinariness just as she can also see herself and Jerry in ironic retrospect as aliens, with him enjoying his apocalyptic visions and 'I myself planning secretly to turn it into black fable and tie it up in my novel, and the town, the people who really were the town, just hooting car horns … and never knowing what danger they were in from us' (*LGW*, 244).

The shock comes when one morning Del meets the real Bobby Sherriff, who invites her into his house for a drink and a piece of cake. Overcome by his courtesy and the ordinariness of everything in the Sherriff house, Del begins to reflect on her Gothic transformations of his family history and discovers what an 'unreliable structure' her unwritten novel actually is. Her perspective shifts radically as she is forced to realise her own limits of vision: 'It is a shock, when you have dealt so cunningly, powerfully, with reality, to come back and find it still there' (*LGW*, 247). As she contemplates the dimensions of secrecy hidden within ordinariness, the young Del is silenced while the story shifts ahead in time to the older Del's perspective, suggesting the kind of novelist she would become. Like her Uncle Craig she would compulsively make lists in her attempts to document the life of Jubilee, though at present 'I didn't look much at this town' (*LGW*, 249). The self ironies multiply at the end as the story returns to the young Del who is surprised by Bobby Sherriff's final odd gesture when he wishes her well and for reasons incomprehensible to her 'rose on his toes like a dancer'. What might have been a joke seems to her more like 'a letter, or a whole word, in an alphabet I did not know'. That gesture, like Barthes's 'punctum', is the crucial supplementary detail which opens up a hitherto 'blind field' and so 'doubles our partial vision.'[22] Del's narrative ends with her later awareness of her adolescent limitations, in a series of doubled perspectives: '"Yes," I said, instead of thank you' (*LGW*, 250).

So we return to the questions at the beginning of this chapter: How to represent a place like Jubilee, and how to map the story of a life like Del's? The answers are already written in the fiction we have just finished reading, though they are only provisional and necessarily incomplete:

> The hope of accuracy we bring to such tasks is crazy, heartbreaking. And no list could hold what I wanted, for what I wanted was every last thing, every layer of speech and thought, stroke of light on bark or walls, every smell, pothole, pain, crack, delusion, held still and held together – radiant, everlasting. (*LGW*, 249)

The book ends with the recognition by one woman writer of her enormous ambition and also of the limits of textual representation, as Del Jordan casts a retrospective glance back at her younger self, noting what she has learned and what she does not yet understand.

Only formal connections:
The Beggar Maid: Stories of Flo and Rose

> Present time and past, the shady melodramatic past of
> Flo's stories, were quite separate, at least for Rose. Present
> people could not be fitted into the past ... As with the
> house, only a formal connection could be made.[1]

IN *The Beggar Maid*, as with *Lives of Girls and Women*,
Munro is concerned with different representations of reality and
the challenge that any one interpretation offers to other possible
interpretations. However, instead of mapping alternative worlds,
this collection focuses not so much on space as on time and how the
past is remembered and reconstructed. The narrator–protagonist in
The Beggar Maid is called Rose. She comes from Hanratty, the
same kind of small country town as Del Jordan's Jubilee, though
Rose's stories deal with a wider range of experience than Del's.
There is less about her childhood and more about her adolescence,
marriage and divorce, while the final story suggests Rose's
ambiguous homecoming as an adult in the late 1970s. Though
the collection is not autobiographical, Munro is writing again
about the place where she grew up and there are shadowy
parallels between the events in Rose's life and her own. Just as in
The Beggar Maid there is a double vision of Hanratty with
earlier and later versions of the town reflected in the time-shifts
within these stories, so Munro commented on her return to
southwestern Ontario after twenty years in British Columbia
that she had a strong awareness of shifts of emphasis within
personal and communal memory over time:

That's one of the things I was talking about. The different editions people make of their lives. So people who could remember these things [the material of Munro's stories] are editing them out.[2]

There is a level at which Munro's stories may be interpreted as documentary realism or as local gossip like the stories that Flo tells Rose, yet other forces are in evidence as well, transforming that referential framework through the powers of imagination. These stories stimulate our awareness of the way that strangeness and ordinariness coexist in everyday life with its 'deep caves paved with kitchen linoleum'.

The opening of 'Royal Beatings' strikingly demonstrates how Munro's protagonists insist on inventing more glorious possibilities than their ordinary lives have to offer. The story recounts Rose's experience at the age of 'nine, ten, eleven, twelve' (BM, 12) when she knows that she is about to receive the most awful hiding from her father:

> *Royal Beating.* That was Flo's promise. You are going to get one Royal Beating.
>
> The word Royal lolled on Flo's tongue, took on trappings. Rose had a need to picture things, to pursue absurdities, that was stronger than the need to stay out of trouble, and instead of taking this threat to heart she pondered: how is a beating royal? She came up with a tree-lined avenue, a crowd of formal spectators, some white horses and black slaves. Someone knelt, and the blood came leaping out like banners. An occasion both savage and splendid. In real life they didn't approach such dignity, and it was only Flo who tried to supply the event with some high air of necessity and regret. Rose and her father soon got beyond anything presentable.
>
> Her father was king of the royal beatings. (BM, 3)

The past leaps out into the present with Rose's vivid memory of her stepmother's voice in the short opening paragraph before shifting into her inner narrative. Right from the start we perceive Rose's peculiar imaginative ability to transform real life into something glamorous and theatrical through her fascination with language: 'how is a beating royal?' However, such slippage from realism encouraged by the voluptuousness of language merely masks for a moment the girl's dread of pain and humiliation, for she knows there will be none of the formality of public ritual when her father beats her. It is a case where private domestic violence parodies and lays bare the brutality of physical punishment. The heroic sits side by side with shabby real life where the contradiction encapsulates the challenge confronting the storyteller. Is it possible to enclose different perceptions of reality within the same textual space where, as Rose realises, 'only a formal connection could be made'? Of course this does not mean that no connections are possible, but it does signal a denial of connections which would be embarrassing or unspeakably painful, just as Rose asserts that 'present people could not be fitted into the past' or 'the person creating noises in the bathroom was not connected with the person who walked out' (*BM*, 6). By 'formal connections' I think Munro means those arrangements that relate to the visible or outward qualities of something, like a patterning of shapes that the narrative might construct according to certain conventions, while recognising that those connections do not necessarily illuminate inward continuities of subjective experience nor do they yield any authoritative meaning. The only meanings available are those constructed by narrative interpretation though every interpretation highlights certain elements and suppresses others. This effort to arrange reality into patterns which gesture provocatively towards hidden connections while at the same time recognising the possible falsity of any fictional construction is what animates Munro's storytelling efforts. What connections can be made between the two different titles under which this collection has always been published? In Canada its title is *Who Do You Think You Are?* while in America and Britain it is *The Beggar Maid: Stories of Flo and Rose*. On Munro's home territory the question 'Who do you think you are?' is commonly used as a reprimand for showing off, and apparently her American publisher objected that this idiom would not be familiar to American readers; Munro agreed to the change although she preferred the Canadian title. It seems to me that more than a change of idiom is at issue here, for the two titles involve different interpretations. *Who Do You Think You Are?* highlights the narrative theme of a female quest and the general response of social disapproval which is provoked by a woman's resistance to traditional expectations. Commenting on this title in an interview over twenty years after writing the book, Munro said:

> I find this very interesting and complicated. I think, in the story, the first time someone says 'Who do you think you are?' it is a teacher reprimanding a student in class, for trying to shine, to show off. I was brought up to think that that is absolutely the worst thing you could do ... So 'Who do you think you are?' comes the minute you begin to let out a little bit of who you would like to be, as soon as you start sort of constructing somebody that is yourself.[3]

Actually the reprimand comes from Flo in the first story and Rose remembers the teacher's words in the last story: 'This was not the first time in her life Rose had been asked who she thought she was' (*BM*, 200). It is a question which becomes increasingly difficult for Rose to answer as she moves away from home to go to university, and then out of her social class through marriage and her later career as radio interviewer and television actress. Rose develops a complex sense of her own identity, always slipping from one persona to another between which 'only formal connections' might be made.

On the other hand, *The Beggar Maid* highlights a particular crisis in Rose's life when she makes the wrong choice in deciding to marry the wealthy postgraduate history student Patrick Blatchford. Munro did not like that title, commenting that it was a very 'still' title which made her think of an historical novel or a fairy tale.[4] Arguably it highlights the fantasy dimension of the book in a way that the other title does not, signalling Patrick's male romantic fantasies about Rose and her lower-class background but also expressing something about Rose herself, for she sees her own desperate longing for love and social acceptance as a kind of beggary. The subtitle is also significant with its focus on Rose's relationship with her stepmother, whose own stories represent the oral tradition of women's gossip which Rose inherits from her.

The Beggar Maid has a similar structural organisation to *Lives* although one is called a collection of short stories and the other a novel. Both belong to the genre of the 'whole book story sequence' where disparate stories are linked through a single narrator's perspective which is refracted in this case in the indirect third-person narrative. Representing stages in Rose's life, these stories revisit the sites of *Lives*, retracing much the same territory though from a different angle of vision which is more highly sensitised to the passage of time. Every story is arranged in sections with time-shifts between sections which are signalled by typographical gaps and often there is a radical time-shift at the end. Here endings function like the Derridean 'supplement' providing a piece of information or an insight which shifts the emphasis and 'throws the whole story line open to question'. (The phrase is taken from 'Simon's Luck', one of the stories in this collection.) Not only does the collection as a whole have a loose open structure but so does every individual story, which works by a series of disarrangements, opening up spaces for new interpretations. Meaning remains contingent on shifting points of view and changing circumstances, though there is always the possibility that there may be dynamic connections between seemingly irreconcilable events. Only by narrative artifice or that old-fashioned word 'composition' can these disparate and often contradictory fragments be arranged into satisfying fictional patterns.

Interestingly, the question of a fictional aesthetic is raised by the story of Munro's manuscript revisions for this book. It is 'the most confused revision in history', as Munro ruefully claimed in her interview with J. R. (Tim) Struthers. Most of the stories had already been published in magazines with heroines of different names ('I often write about the same heroine and give her a different name ... But her psychological make-up is not different').[5] When Munro submitted the new collection to her Canadian publisher in 1978 under the title *Rose and Janet* there were two heroines, each with her own group of stories.

Then, when the book was at first page-proofs stage she decided to write two new Rose stories ('Who Do You Think You Are?' and 'Simon's Luck') and with that came the sudden concept-ualising of this volume. Munro withdrew the book at her own expense and substantially rewrote it.[6] It won a Governor General's Award for Fiction in Canada and was shortlisted for the Booker Prize in Britain.

It is within a performance context that this autobiographical fiction should be read. Is it a quest for the self? Not in any simple sense, for Rose has great difficulty in defining herself as a subject. Hers is a quest to construct a self-image which will accommodate her shifting aspirations and desires as she end-lessly reinvents herself in response to changing circumstances.[7] As she confesses in the last story, speaking about her old school friend Ralph Gillespie and his comic impersonations of local characters, she too has a longing to be a mimic: 'She wanted to fill up in that magical, releasing way, transform herself; she wanted the courage and the power'(BM, 204). Theatricality and fantasy are pervasive as Rose watches herself and other people acting roles in real-life dramas like the sort of improvised theatre that is represented in 'Royal Beatings'. Her profession as actress highlights the artifice involved in creating a self-image as she rehearses multiple images of herself at different ages in her ironic retrospective narrative. Again Munro is presenting female subjectivity as a highly complex network of conscious and unconscious desires and fears, and it may be helpful to remember what another critic says of Munro's fiction: 'the single self finds a reflection in what is not: in thoughts, emotions, pictures, signs – the world, in other words of "images"'.[8] Only through impersonation, fantasies and a variety of provisional structures can the self be figured at all, and then it is only a partial oversimplified image which appears.

What kind of stories does Rose tell about herself? She presents herself as a marginalised figure living in the poorest part of Hanratty, yet with intelligence and ambition and the desire for a life closer to the scandalous flamboyancy of Flo's stories. She is always unsettling her relation to the traditional images of femininity to which she is expected to conform. This rehearsal of difference is analogous to Munro's own shifts of emphasis in her storytelling methods, where the limits of realism are subverted even while her stories work within the realistic mode. Rose's fantasising coexists with her normal everyday living for the possibilities envisaged by her as actress and fantasist do not exist outside reality; instead, they are hidden within it.

The stories I have chosen for close analysis demonstrate the distinctive mixture of realism, theatricality and fantasy which characterises Rose's life narrative as she enacts her dramas of identity. 'Royal Beatings' is in many ways a dress rehearsal for the major themes in this book, showing Rose's childhood fascination with language and her conflictual relationship with her father and stepmother as well as her imaginative sense of the hidden mysteries below social surfaces. 'The Beggar Maid' and 'Simon's Luck' provide two versions of romantic fantasy which belong to different periods in Rose's life: in the first, Rose is a bright young university student from a poor background while in the second she is a divorcee in her thirties who works as an actress. Though different in form, one being a version of the Cinderella story and the other of a deserted woman, they are both fixated on that same moment of transformation through sexual love which all Munro's heroines fantasise about. The final story 'Who Do You Think You Are?' functions like 'Epilogue: The Photographer' (*LGW*), making its metafictional comment on the whole collection. This is a shared feature of these two texts which we shall not find in Munro's later collections, though we may trace its gradual attenuation through *The Moons of Jupiter* and *The Progress of Love* to its disappearance in *Friend of My Youth* and *Open Secrets*. As Rose looks back at her life connections are shown to be more than formal, though only if she looks below the surface into the subtext which is normally hidden by conventional discourse.

Munro has often remarked on the 'Gothic' quality of life in the small town where she grew up in the 1930s and 1940s with its mixture of the ordinary and the bizarre:

It's a rural culture with a strong Scots–Irish background.
With a big sense of righteousness. But with big bustings-
out and grotesque crime. And ferocious sexual humour and
the habit of getting drunk and killing each other off on the
roads. There's always this sort of boiling life going on.[9]

This is exactly the scenario which is represented in Munro's
early fictions and 'Royal Beatings' continues the pattern. Like
the opening story of *Lives* it offers a representation of Rose's
childhood world: her family and her home, their social situation
and local scandals. It also situates this world in a historical frame
which includes the adult Rose's retrospective view from the
distance of Toronto and goes back a hundred years before that to
the days of pioneer settlement, ironising any nostalgia for the
good old days. In realistic terms the incident in 'Royal Beatings'
might well be seen as a case of child abuse where a girl is beaten
by her father, though it is transformed by the narrative into a
bizarre performance. Indeed, the beating seen from the child's
point of view is highly theatrical, for Rose sees her father
looking 'like a bad actor, who turns a part grotesque ... That is
not to say he is pretending, that he is acting, and does not mean
it. He is acting, and he means it. Rose knows that, she knows
everything about him'(*BM*, 18).

With all her faculties sharpened by fear Rose has a terrible
flash of insight into the contradictory nature of reality, into that
'treachery' which is 'the other side of dailiness' (*BM*, 19), as she
realises that her usually gentle father is taking a sadistic pleasure
in hurting her, working himself up into it. She wonders later
about murder and whether murderers might at some level be
motivated by a similarly transgressive impulse: 'Does the thing
have to be carried through, in the end, partly for the effect, to
prove to the audience of one ... that there is nothing that can't
happen, that the most dreadful antic is justified, feelings can be
found to match it' (*BM*, 18). Rose also realises her own complicity
in her beating and her masochistic pleasure as she plays the role
of her father's victim. Why does she have to 'play her part in
this with the same grossness, the same exaggeration, that her
father displays, playing his?' (*BM*, 19). They do of course have

an audience in Flo, who has initiated the whole exercise and who now stands appalled at the consequences. Rose and her father both go on to the point of exhaustion – after which family life can gradually return to normal. It is as if that outburst of savagery provides a kind of catharsis, and they all feel better afterwards. They all slip back into their usual roles with less embarrassment than might have been expected. Again, only formal connections can be made between Rose's two fathers: 'The two persons were not the same, though they seemed to occupy the same space' (*BM*, 6).

Munro's narrative brings another perspective to bear on the beating which takes it beyond Rose's family context, for the story is set within the frame of Flo's terrible story about the crippled girl Becky Tyde, an abused child (whose father beat her and according to local gossip, made pregnant) and the horse-whipping of old Mr Tyde by three young men from the town. That too was like a performance with Becky as a child in her nightgown watching through the window as her father lay bleeding on the snow. That story is one of the town's open secrets which everybody knows but which nobody refers to. Here it is Flo's story, so that Flo is implicated in both these Royal Beatings as teller and as instigator. The two beatings are conflated and comment on each other at the end, when 'many years later' Rose in Toronto hears a radio interview with Hat Nettleton on his 102nd birthday from the Wawanash County Home for the Aged and she thinks: 'Hat Nettleton. Horsewhipper into Centenarian' (*BM*, 24). Flo herself is by then in that same county home and Rose has the urge to tell her about it. However that is no longer possible for Flo has stopped talking or listening, 'though she occasionally showed her feelings by biting a nurse' (*BM*, 24). The final Royal Beating is death, but what the story does is to keep a lot of forgotten feelings in circulation. They go on haunting the memories of the survivors and in Rose's case are transformed into an important masochistic element in her romantic fantasies.

The two stories dealing with romantic fantasy, 'The Beggar Maid' and 'Simon's Luck', relate Munro's fiction to the traditional subject matter of women's novels while at the same time her treatment shows her ironic revision of popular romance plots. Munro writes very well about the banality and the power of fantasy, which remains a central fact not affected by age or gender but which provides an inner space in which to invent new images of the self. She is very interested in erotic fantasies as an urgent part of sexual experience for women as well as men and in those shadowy areas where male and female fantasies appear to mesh together though actually they contradict each other.

This is the territory which she explores in 'The Beggar Maid', which begins: 'Patrick Blatchford was in love with Rose. This had become a fixed, even furious, idea with him. For her, a continual surprise. He wanted to marry her' (*BM*, 68). The story is far more about Patrick's fantasy than it is about that of Rose, who continues to vacillate between complicity and resistance. It had all started with a savage joke when an unknown man grabbed Rose's leg in the library stacks and she rushed over to tell a studious young graduate student what had happened: 'That was Patrick. If she had been trying to make him fall in love with her there was no better way she could have chosen' (*BM*, 77). Rose's plight happens to fit exactly into Patrick's chivalrous fantasies about rescuing damsels in distress and he adopts her into his imaginary world. He even discovers her image in a painting, Sir Edward Burne-Jones's Pre-Raphaelite picture *King Cophetua and the Beggar Maid* (1884), transforming Rose's identity according to a principle of male discourse which is described precisely by Irigaray: 'Reality appears as an always already cultural reality, linked to the individual and collective history of the masculine subject'.[10] Patrick chooses a male painter's image of the ideal feminine as 'meek and voluptuous' and submissive to male power. If Rose is the Beggar Maid, then who could Patrick be except King Cophetua gazing in rapture at her? He sees himself as the heroic rescuer who has the power and the will to transform her into his Queen (echoing the last line of Tennyson's poem 'The Beggar Maid'). No wonder Rose is made uneasy by this painting when she looks it up in an art book in the library! Seeing it from a woman's perspective she does not like this image of helpless femininity and 'milky surrender'. Taking her distance from the male gaze in the painting, Rose perceives the sexual politics coded into it just as she sees right through Patrick's power fantasy:

> Was that how Patrick saw Rose? Was that how she could be? She would need that king, sharp and swarthy as he looked ... He could make a puddle of her, with his fierce desire. There would be no apologizing with him. (*BM*, 80)

Again, as in 'Royal Beatings' Rose compares the heroic ideal with the human reality and she is left floundering in the enormous gap that opens up between them.

Why, we may ask, does Rose agree to marry Patrick? The answer would seem to be that at an emotional level she truly is a beggar maid needing to be loved and worshipped, just as her more worldly self is attracted by the image of social prestige which this marriage offers: 'It was a miracle; it was a mistake. It was what she had dreamed of; it was not what she wanted' (*BM*, 81). This is a significant variant on the female fantasy of total submission to the beloved as for Rose it is a power fantasy, and she enters into it as an actress: 'The deceits and stratagems were only hers; Patrick was never a fraud' (*BM*, 84). The trouble with fantasy is that it leaves so much out:

> What about all the rest of her? Energy, laziness, vanity, discontent, ambition? She concealed all that. He had no idea. For all her doubts about him, she never wanted him to fall out of love with her. (*BM*, 86)

Their ten-year marriage is a disaster, and finally Rose leaves her husband and their daughter Anna to go to work at a radio station and later becomes a television actress.

The final section is set at nine years' distance from their divorce, when Rose and Patrick see each other late one night by accident at Toronto airport; Patrick pulls a horrible face at her, as if he had seen in her his *'true enemy'* (*BM*, 99). His grotesque gesture of 'disgust and loathing' in this almost surreal scene spells out the aftermath of romantic fantasy and its betrayal. His 'love' of the first section has turned to 'hate' in the last, signalling in that melodramatic language a subtext of unspeakable feelings of hurt and humiliation – and Rose is as surprised by Patrick's loathing as she ever was by his love. Again, all the contradictory pieces sit side by side and only formal connections can be made: indeterminacy has become the principle within the narrative structure as within the relationship between Rose and Patrick.

Rose never grows out of romantic fantasy and 'Simon's Luck' offers a later version where Rose, now in her late thirties after a divorce and several abortive affairs,[11] falls in love once again, this time with a European Jewish classics lecturer called Simon whom she meets at a party. Again it is a woman's fantasy about desire for rescue through love, but this time it is the opposite of a power fantasy. There is a strong subtext here of Rose's secret scenarios of loneliness, humiliations and her fear of ageing, together with her unspoken guilts and her need for forgiveness. Simon spends one enchanted weekend with Rose but he never returns and she makes herself utterly miserable waiting for him, before chasing after him hundreds of miles by car. The most interesting comment on romantic fantasy here is the scrutiny of a woman's changing state of mind as Rose falls out of love during her car trip. The moment of climactic change happens when Rose walks into a café early one morning in a small prairie town, only to find herself overwhelmed by the ordinariness of everything: 'It was those dishes that told her of her changed state ... she saw them in a way that wouldn't be possible to a person in any stage of love' (BM, 175).

Though 'Rose-tinted spectacles' would be a bad pun, the idea of distorted vision does apply to Rose's recognition that being in love is a kind of fantasy state which 'removes the world for you'. Rose realises that by seeing her predicament through clichéd images of female helplessness, she has allowed love to rob her of her 'private balance spring, a little dry kernel of probity' which is the nearest that Munro ever comes to defining a subjective centre of being for her protagonists.

It is with Rose's recognition of the seductiveness of romantic fantasy and her return to the reassuring intransigence of real life that the doubled structure of the story becomes apparent.

There are two stories in conflict here with Rose's romantic fantasy narrative embedded in her realistic narrative. Each follows different literary conventions and only formal connections can be made between them. This duality is highlighted by the time-shift at the end which gives a shocking new twist to the plot. 'A year or so later' when Rose is working in a television soap on location in British Columbia, she learns that Simon has died, which casts a new light on the possible reasons why he never returned. Confronted with the news of his death and the information that he was dying of cancer at the time when she knew him, Rose suddenly sees that real life does not conform to fantasy plots. Happy endings are available for certain only in soap operas, which filter out bewildering contingencies according to specific literary conventions. Compared with real life their 'realism' is merely spurious and consolatory.[12] Rose has been following the wrong plot, and only at the end is she forced to realise that vulnerability and the humiliations of the body are not her own special prerogatives:

> It was preposterous, it was unfair, that such a chunk of information should have been left out, and that Rose even at this late date could have thought herself the only person who could seriously lack power. (*BM*, 177)

The final story 'Who Do You Think You Are?' has a similar function to the last story in *Lives*. Like 'Epilogue: The Photographer' it offers a wider perspective on the protagonist and a sense of an ending, for this is the story where Rose comes home. 'Who Do You Think You Are?' is obsessed with homecomings and anecdotes about Hanratty in the past and in the present, for despite Rose's nomadic tendencies she has a strong sense of local attachment and a profound unease about her past so that she is always going back to revisit the sites of old traumas. The retrospective narrative makes space to accommodate several kinds of history: the local history of Hanratty with its eccentric characters, changes in the townscape over forty years, and also Rose's personal history with its memories slipping back to childhood. The main Hanratty 'character' here is Milton Homer, introduced in the first sentence of the story: 'There were some things Rose and her brother Brian could safely talk about, without running aground on principles or statements of position, and one of them was Milton Homer' (*BM*, 193). Curiously, as it develops, the story becomes precisely a statement of Rose's position in relation to her past just as it provides the nearest thing she gets (or we get) to an answer to the question posed by its title. Focused on issues of identity, this story constructs a concept of the self which, though it evades definition, may be located in relationship to community. The narrative moves towards a sense of connection in almost linear fashion, tracing the range of shadow selves and theatrical personae through which Rose comes to recognise herself in sameness and difference.

Milton Homer was the town eccentric of Rose's childhood, whose unofficial public function it was to 'march in parades', mocking the ceremonies of social order in Hanratty. He was not the 'village idiot' as one outsider called him, for Hanratty was not a village and Milton Homer was not an idiot, though his lack of any sense of social inhibition made him a grotesquely comic figure. His position was the traditional one of licensed fool. During the annual Orange Walk,

> He could show up anywhere in the parade and he varied his place in it from time to time ... Behind the Black Knights he would pull a dour face, and hold his head as if a top hat was riding on it; behind the ladies he wiggled his hips and diddled an imaginary sunshade. He was a mimic of ferocious gifts and terrible energy. (*BM*, 196)

If Milton Homer is one of the ferocious mimics in this story, then Rose is another and so was her classmate Ralph Gillespie, whose trademark it was to do imitations of Milton Homer, while Rose in turn did imitations of Ralph 'doing Milton Homer.' Rose, Ralph, and Milton Homer as three of a kind – all outsiders in their different ways, with a keen sense of irreverence and absurdity and all with the same transgressive delight in performance. The main difference between them is that while Milton could not help 'his goggling leering drooping looks',

Rose and Ralph deliberately set out to make spectacles of themselves for public entertainment.

It is as if only by pulling faces and by becoming someone else through acting a role could they be freed 'to let out a little bit of who they would like to be'. Seeing Ralph at school doing his Milton Homer imitation, Rose 'wanted to fill up in that magical, releasing way, transform herself, she wanted the courage and the power' (*BM*, 204). The relation between Rose and Ralph is at the centre of this story, and their meeting again after many years marks Rose's moment of homecoming. By the time they meet again at the Legion Hall in Hanratty, Flo is in the Wawanash County Home (where Milton Homer has already died like Hat Nettleton before him), Rose is a successful actress in Toronto, and Ralph is back home having been invalided out of the Navy. Their meeting is an important one for Rose because it shows her that connections are sometimes more than formal: after so many years, they can still share 'the same silent joke, the same conspiracy, comfort; the same, the same' (*BM*, 209). Their conversation, though not particularly satisfactory, manages to alleviate Rose's peculiar sense of shame which she always feels as an artist:

> The thing she was ashamed of, in acting, was that she might have been paying attention to the wrong things, reporting antics, when there was always something further, a tone, a depth, a light, that she couldn't get and wouldn't get. And it wasn't just about acting that she suspected this. (*BM*, 209)

With Ralph, Rose does not have to play-act or construct romantic fantasies for their intimacy is not based on love or sex; instead, Ralph is Rose's mirror image, reflecting back her own qualities and granting her the forgiveness for transgression which she cannot give to herself. The connection between them is so close that Rose feels Ralph's life is only 'one slot over from her own' (*BM*, 210). That spatial metaphor is important, for their encounter gives Rose at last a sense of her 'place' which goes back past all her changing identities into her childhood.

It is significant that Rose decides for once not to say anything to anybody about Ralph or about the later news of his accidental death, 'glad that there was one thing at least that she wouldn't spoil by telling' (BM, 210). And that brings me to an important point about Munro's fictions which is implicit in Rose's comments about her acting and her obscure sense of shame, for Munro fears the same kind of treachery in her writing: 'Even as I most feverishly practise it, I am a little afraid that the work with words may turn out to be a questionable trick, an evasion … an unavoidable lie.'[13] This kind of moral anxiety behind the delight in artifice brings about a curious elision between Rose's perspective and Munro's own when the narrative voice speaks about the wisdom of keeping quiet:

> There seemed to be feelings which could only be spoken of in translation … not speaking of them and not acting on them is the right course to take because translation is dubious. Dangerous, as well. (BM, 210)

These stories told by Flo and Rose – and by Munro – all attempt to 'translate' reality into fiction. Reality however is always excessive and full of unaccommodated remainders, which is why these stories are made of fragments and gaps – 'all the things you can't know about'. There is always room in the gaps for other possible connections to be made as well as for secrets, those things that should not be spoiled by telling.

Star maps and shifting perspectives:
The Moons of Jupiter

> Clear nights, with Roberta pointing out to him the
> unlikely ways the stars tie up into their constellations, and
> every day pure gold ... She seemed to him courageous,
> truthful, without vanity. How out of this could come such
> touchiness, tearfulness, weariness, such a threat of
> collapse he cannot imagine.[1]

ALICE Munro's fiction has always been concerned with
mapping locations and charting shifts in perspective which
'throw the storyline open to question' (*BM*, 177), but the
dazzling shift in the sketch above from celestial maps traced in
the night sky to a man's failure of imagination at the prospect of
a woman's imminent emotional collapse a year later suggest
new departures in her fifth collection of stories published in
1982. *The Moons of Jupiter* is arguably the most significant
turning point in Munro's fiction-writing career, for it signals a
radical change in her storytelling methods as she develops new
ways of writing the passage of time, moving out into a vast
cosmological frame of reference where the stories play between
the polarities of the cosmic and the everyday. The very title of
this collection indicates a shift away from maps of the earth to
maps of the heavens, together with associated concepts of
dynamic change and indeterminate meanings held in ceaseless
circulation. The Moons of Jupiter analogy is significant, though
I would like to reassure readers that these stories do not operate
in the stratosphere. On the contrary, as the narrator in the title
story remarks on observing the schoolchildren's reactions to the

show at the Toronto Planetarium: 'An effort had been made to get their attention, to take it away from canned pop and potato chips and fix it on various knowns and unknowns and horrible immensities, and it seemed to have failed. A good thing, too, I thought'(*MJ*, 231).

Munro continues to locate her stories in familiar places. They all begin with the social landscapes of small Canadian towns and the surrounding countryside of southwestern Ontario which she has represented to her readers from the beginning. Her subject matter remains familiar too: Canadian pioneer history which is also local history and family history, relationships within families and between generations, and perhaps most importantly, the relationships between men and women. As Munro remarked in an interview with Geoff Hancock on the eve of the publication of *Moons*, 'Well, that's the main thing isn't it? This is endlessly interesting and you keep discovering more things about it as a person and as a writer. The whole subject of what men and women want of each other. The big drama of life as I see it right now.'[2] Her topics have not changed but her narrative methods have. No longer do these stories sit like 'pictures hanging together' as they did in *Lives of Girls and Women*, for such a static conception is replaced by a model of endless motion where instability of meaning within any individual story is complemented by the mobile arrangement of the collection as a whole as stories 'orbit' around one another in shifting relationships analogous with the apparently erratic gravitational patterns of the satellites of the planet Jupiter.[3]

The new mobility of conception is apparent in this sequence of eleven stories; they do not present the map of a single life (as in *Lives* or *The Beggar Maid*) but instead a 'star map' of many women's lives, each spinning on its own axis yet brought by the narrative design into patterns of relationship. When the focus shifts as it so often does, these lives rotate off into darkness as their own independent life cycles continue. Only the first and last stories share the same narrator; she is that 'Janet Fleming' character whose stories Munro separated from Rose's at the last minute in her revisions of *The Beggar Maid*.[4] The other nine stories are told (sometimes in the first person and sometimes in the third) by a variety of women of widely differing ages, from young girls to women in their forties and fifties and even in their eighties, where every woman's story provides a new perspective on all the others. Although the details of every woman's life story are different, they share common experiences like falling in love, getting married, having children, ageing and dying, so that the focus shifts continually between particularities and universal patterns. With an emphasis on the changes wrought by time on women's bodies and their lives, these stories represent 'innumerable repetitions, innumerable variations' in the feminine experience. That phrase comes from the title story where the narrator is referring to the stars and planets in the galaxy as they roll past her head 'like balls of lightning' in the planetarium (*MJ*, 231). The 'barely felt gravitational pulls and ironic repulsions'[5] between characters and stories are a function of the overall narrative design which suggests a wider dynamic transcending any individual's experience, though it is only in the last story that the frame of reference becomes explicitly cosmological and mythic.

In every story the narrator's point of view and her frames of reference shift over time, so that events are always being repositioned and re-evaluated: 'Mostly in my stories I like to look at what people don't understand. What we don't understand. What we think is happening and what we understand later on, and so on.'[6] The stories are divided into sections with typographical spaces between sections. While there is no unifying plot, there is always a central point of reference to which all the parts relate through processes of memory and association, adding layers of meaning which accumulate around that central point. Returning to the Moons of Jupiter analogy, we could describe these stories as being structured on a 'centre and orbiting' principle; this is the model which my analysis of individual stories will follow.[7] Such structures of layered digressions preserve the apparent randomness of experience while rearranging the details of real life into patterns, so that both the narrator and the reader see things that were previously invisible. When we come to the overall arrangement, we see a linear patterning from stories of origin to stories of deaths and endings while along the way stories chart the riddles and mysteries of everyday life. Munro's storytelling methods have always encouraged a plurality of meanings as alternative worlds are positioned 'alongside' each other in the same geographical and fictional space, but here a new dimension is introduced as maps of landscape are overlaid by the mobile maps of cosmology or the indecipherable codes of destiny.

A remarkable example of this new speculative textual mapping occurs in 'Labor Day Dinner' where Roberta and George, the couple who watched the constellations referred to in my opening quotation, are driving home from a dinner party late at night 'down the third concession road of Weymouth Township, known locally as the Telephone Road' (MJ, 158) when they are almost run into by a 'dark-green 1969 Dodge travelling at between eighty and ninety miles an hour' approaching from a side road. The crisis is silent and swift as

> the big car flashes before them, a huge, dark flash, without lights, seemingly without sound. It comes out of the dark corn and fills the air right in front of them the way a big flat fish will glide into view suddenly in an aquarium tank … Then it's gone – it has disappeared into the corn on the other side of the road. They drive on. (MJ, 159)

Despite the documentary detail – or perhaps because of it – the reader's response to this missed encounter is probably the same as Roberta and George's: 'What they feel is not terror or thanks-giving – not yet. What they feel is strangeness' (MJ, 159). This particular road grid in southwestern Ontario is suddenly over-laid in darkness with an entirely different and indecipherable pattern signalled by the near accident; the sense of strangeness comes from the apprehension of the crossing of one pattern by another which seems to belong to a different dimension. The stories are pervaded by their narrators' awareness of partial knowledge, deferrals of meaning and speculations on the patterns of destiny coded into astronomy, astrology and myth.

I would also like to point to the feminine order of meaning which Munro privileges here as she displaces the emphasis from Jupiter to the spinning satellites. Indeed there is no mention of Jupiter at all till the final story for the focus is on mothers and aunts rather than on fathers and grandfathers, with stories told from the women's points of view. In the first story Janet rewrites 'Heirs of the Living Body' (*LGW*, 28–62) telling the stories of the women in her family which have been buried under the claims of stories by and about men. Here patriarchal figures are often discredited, while traditionally feminine positions are shown to be restrictive and damaging or at best cherished romantic illusions. It is only in the title story which is Janet's elegy for her father that mutual love and understanding is acknowledged, at the same time as Jupiter is finally named. I shall discuss these two stories plus two others, 'Accident' and 'Bardon Bus', both of which appear to follow erratic orbits of their own in their different versions of women's romantic fantasies. Yet from another perspective these stories look like mirror images of each other and are subject to the same 'barely felt gravitational pulls' which operate across the whole collection.

Munro's stories may be situated within a realistic frame of reference, though she is always concerned with the shifting significance of events when viewed from different locations in time and circumstance. 'Chaddeleys and Flemings' is a mirror story in two parts representing the double strain in Janet Fleming's inheritance, for her grandparents and great-grandparents emigrated from England and Scotland to Canada in the mid-nineteenth century. It is within this awareness of history that Janet looks back in the late 1970s to the 1940s at two important visits in her childhood. The first story 'Connection' centres on a summer visit made by her maternal aunts to her family in the small town of Dalgleish, and the second story 'The Stone in the Field' turns to another summer visit made by Janet's family to her paternal aunts on the farm where they and her father grew up. One story faces outwards from Dalgleish to the wider world while the other faces inwards to the secret lives of the unmarried sisters on the farm who, as Janet's modern mother opines, 'belonged in another generation' (*MJ*, 22). In both stories Janet's memories flow in and around her thoughts in the present as she registers changes and continuities between the living and the dead.

The boisterous arrival of the four Chaddeley aunts, worldly unmarried women who drive cars and smoke cigarettes, introduces a note of the carnivalesque into the routines of family life in Dalgleish. Their visit reaches its climax in the impromptu concert where even Janet's mother takes part: 'My mother, most amazingly, put on a pair of my father's trousers and stood on her head'(*MJ*, 4). To a young girl like Janet, the aunts are transforming presences, just as their stories about their English grandfather ('What an old snob he was, they said, but how handsome even as an old man, what a carriage,' *MJ*, 8) transform the past into the stuff of legend:

> Connection, that was what it was all about. The cousins ... provided a connection. A connection with the real, and prodigal, and dangerous, world ... The other connection they provided, and my mother provided as well, was to England and history. (*MJ*, 6–7)

Janet with her divided inheritance cannot totally sympathise with these pretensions even at the time, and she lives to see through this legend when years later she learns about her great-grandfather's true origins. (Joseph Ellington Chaddeley had been a butcher's apprentice, not an Oxford student who had run into debt, as Janet's aunts and her mother had fondly imagined.)

Just as the story registers changing interpretations of family history, so the narrative method registers Janet's own changing angles of vision over time. As she says,

> At one time I would have been shocked to discover this ... At another, later, time, when I was dedicated to tearing away all false notions, all illusions, I would have been triumphant. By the time the revelation came I did not care, one way or the other. (*MJ*, 10)

We are reminded that this is also a fictive autobiography told by a woman who believes that she has put her past behind her, only to find old events and feelings being recycled at a later time and in another place in parodic form and with disastrous consequences. When Cousin Iris, now retired and alone, visits Janet and her prosperous lawyer husband in Vancouver, the husband ridicules her as a 'pathetic old tart', whereupon Janet's buried family loyalties burst out in grotesque form: she throws the dish with the remains of a lemon meringue pie in it at his head. This farcical scene is oddly reminiscent of the Dalgleish concert, or as Janet remarks, like something out of an *I Love Lucy* show, though the effect is quite different as two incongruities jar against each other. This time they produce amazement (just like her mother's circus trick all those years earlier) but now it is 'amazement, that something people invariably thought funny in those instances should be so shocking a verdict in real life' (*MJ*, 18). By the time she is telling this story Janet is divorced and her mother and the aunts are all dead, so that in the final section when the past is retrieved yet again, Janet sees the aunts from a different angle entirely as she hears in memory the round that they sang on their summer visit to Dalgleish. Now the sound seems to thin out over time from four voices to only one, signalling the dissolution of all that had seemed so solid and reassuring to the child:

> *Merrily, merrily, merrily, merrily,*
> *Life is but a dream.* (*MJ*, 18)

The same elegiac note is sounded in the companion piece 'The Stone in the Field' as it maps shifting perspectives and losses on the other side of the family. Her father's side represents the dour Scottish pioneer ethic of which Janet is also the inheritor, and as the story winds its way through the maze of country roads in southwestern Ontario on a Sunday afternoon back to the old Fleming farm it also figures a journey back in time. The young girl registers the texture of that old fashioned house and the condition of these countrywomen's restricted lives:

> The room was cleaner and barer than any I have ever been in. There was no sign of frivolity, no indication that the people who lived here ever sought entertainment ... Work

would be what filled their lives, not conversation; work would be what gave their days shape. (*MJ*, 26)

Theirs is a sealed-off life which keeps its secrets, and it is only during her father's last illness long after his sisters are dead that Janet has any insight at all into their history, when he tells her about her Scottish grandfather and the harsh lives of the early settlers. He also tells her a story about an Austrian immigrant called Mr Black who lived during her grandfather's time in a shack on the farm land and was buried there under an unmarked boulder.

In what we recognise as a characteristic time shift ('some time after my father died') Janet comes again upon the story of Mr Black's death from 'a cancer of the tongue' in an old newspaper clipping in the Toronto Library. So she goes back to the farm, only to find everything has changed. The roads have been straightened, the old house has been transformed and the new owners have a different lifestyle from her paternal aunts: 'I said that a farmer was just like a businessman nowadays, wasn't he?' (*MJ*, 34). Not surprisingly, just as times and farming methods have changed so has the map, and the stone cannot be found: 'He said that of course the corner of a field then was not necessarily the corner of a field now'(*MJ*, 35). The story ends with Janet's mapping her range of possible responses to Mr Black's fragmented narrative:

> If I had been younger, I would have figured out a story [a romance] ... Later ... I would have made a horrible, plausible connection between that silence of his, and the manner of his death. Now I no longer believe that people's secrets are defined and communicable, or their feelings full blown and easy to recognize. (*MJ*, 35)

Her multiple interpretations serve as a metafictional comment on the way that an artist might use the raw materials of history, suggesting the many reconstructions that could be made from the same incomplete evidence. This is a narrative strategy which Munro perfects in this collection and which she uses again in many later stories.

Finally Janet comes to see herself in a new relation to her double inheritance, 'the whole solid, intricate structure of lives supporting us from the past' as Del had described it in *Lives* (*LGW*, 31). However, for Janet the solidity has vanished: some things are irretrievably lost, the dead do keep their secrets, and only traces of the past survive in the present: 'However they behaved they are all dead. I carry something of them around in me' (*MJ*, 35). There are as many changes and transformations in families as there have been in the landscape and the story ends with a reference to the vanished burial stone and a respectful refusal to indulge in nostalgia for pioneer days: 'The life buried here is one you have to think twice about regretting' (*MJ*, 35). Though powerfully elegiac, these stories cannot be confined to that genre alone, for they are also chronicles of the inevitability of change as well as its necessity; people and things that seemed so solid and fixed as if they would 'go on forever' (this phrase occurs in both stories) are shown not to be like that at all. One story ends with the word 'dream' and the other with the recognition that the same spaces of earth are occupied differently by later generations, as Munro writes the passage of time. Much later, in an interview in 1994 after *Open Secrets* was published Munro said,

> The older I get, the more I see things as having more than one explanation. I see the content of life as being many layered. And in a way, nothing that happens really takes precedence over anything else that happens.[8]

In the same interview she also said that she sought through her stories 'to find something that was in a way always the same, no matter what incidental forms life took'. That double awareness of endless process and of the significance of individual experience provides both the context of inquiry and the connecting link between the first story and all the others.

'Accident' is a version of the female romance plot though it is also a story about the role that chance plays in people's lives, for (unlike 'Labor Day Dinner') there is a fatal accident here with the death of a nine-year-old boy whose sledge is pushed under a car one wintry December afternoon in 1943 in the small town of Hanratty. The story does not begin with that event however but with the love affair between a young high-school music teacher Frances Wright and the science master Ted Makkavala, the boy's father. As the story develops, arbitrariness so pervades the action that we begin to wonder if there are not two accidents here: the road accident and the romance itself, for even Frances suspects that it may be 'a rickety invention' (*MJ*, 79), the product of circumstance and her own desire for adventure. Both these 'accidents' have far-reaching though unpredictable consequences, and the story traces the interwoven effects of both events over a period of thirty years up to the late 1970s when Frances, long since married to Ted and now the mother of two daughters, returns to her home town for her sister-in-law's funeral. Glancing back over her life, Frances fails to find in it any meaningful pattern at all.

Munro's story again exploits shifting perspectives as it relates events from Frances's and Ted's differing points of view, sometimes in the present and sometimes in the past tense, though always indirectly so that the reader has the sense of being an onlooker who is missing some vital clue. What is clear however is that Ted's vaunted scientific rational view of the world offers no more explanation for the contingencies of life than Frances's subjectivised feminine perceptions. (We may recall that Aristotle in his *Metaphysics* suggested that there 'was no science of the accidental at all'.)[9] Frances's life story would appear to conform in broad outline to the conventions of a romance plot where she falls in love with a dark stranger and their transgressive love affair is finally resolved in marriage after a death and a divorce. Yet the story is infinitely more disturbing than this, for at every turn the design is interrupted to reveal fragments of other repressed stories which are at odds with Frances's version – Ted's Finnish wife's narrative for example, his anecdotes from his past life before he met Frances, and Frances's own scepticism about the very romance plot she has invented for herself. Indeed when Ted unexpectedly makes his proposal of marriage (having come to the decision on the spur of the moment when arguing with the head master) this declaration which is traditionally the climax of a love story is so overshadowed by anxiety that Frances is quite terrified at her sudden vision of helplessness and insignificance:

> There was a long chain of things, many of them hidden from her, that brought him here to propose to her in the most proper place, her mother's living room. She had been made necessary ... Because it [the chain] was linked as it was. (*MJ*, 106–7)

This version of the impersonal operations of destiny where lives are arbitrarily forced into convergence so radically challenges the figurings of desire in the romance plot that perhaps the question we should be asking here is the one which Gillian Beer asked of the stories of George Eliot and Virginia Woolf': 'Can the female self be expressed through plot or must it be conceived in resistance to plot?'[10] Certainly there are determining events in Frances's life, but they only become so when seen in retrospect; at the time they appear 'accidental'. Frances herself is always aware of her position as outsider. She is alone at the beginning, 'loitering' outside the science room where she has no business to be; she is alone after the accident when Ted goes with his wife to the hospital to sit by his dying son; and she is an outsider at the end when she returns to Hanratty for her sister-in-law's funeral. More disconcerting perhaps is Frances's double vision of her own life, where she is continually coming up against perceptions that do not bear looking into any more than the bottles of biological specimens in the science supply room at school where she and Ted make love – like her doubts about her romance with its flashes of 'dismay and disappointment that she would not listen to' (*MJ*, 86). Marriage is not the centre of Frances's story, for those details are pushed to the margins as it leaps ahead thirty years to her retrospective glance over her life when she stands greeting people at the Hanratty Funeral Home. Frances finds herself wondering what would have happened if Bobby Makkavala had not been killed. Would she have ever married Ted, or would she have remained in Hanratty teaching music, or would she have gone elsewhere? Suddenly her perception shifts sharply as she turns away from those unlived possibilities, in a circling back to 'something that was in a way always the same' – something very close to an essential self:

> *What difference*, thinks Frances ... of course there is a difference, anybody can see that, a life's difference ... But inside she's ticking away, all by herself, the same Frances who was there before any of it.
>
> Not altogether the same, surely.
>
> The same.
>
> I'll be as bad as Mother when I get old, she thinks, turning eagerly to greet somebody. Never mind. She has a way to go yet. (*MJ*, 109)

The story ends at a point beyond romance for it is played out as one woman's hidden resistance to the plot of her own life story. Far from being a split self, Frances is a self split off from the world and surviving behind her changing social masks. Indeed, this narrative of a self untransformed by love, sex, scandal, marriage, children or the death of others threatens the chilling possibility of death, not only of romantic plots but of narrative itself, when the events of real life are reduced to 'accidents' or 'the incidental forms that life took'.

'Bardon Bus' appears to offer a very different version of female romance, weaving together a series of failed love affairs as two women compulsively reinvent themselves in their desire to find emotional and sexual fulfilment. But how different is it really? Certainly the angle of vision is different:

> In a story called 'Bardon Bus' I want to have a kind of feeling of hysterical eroticism. Very edgy and sad. This came to me from the feelings I get sometimes in women's dress shops. It's a feeling about the masquerades and attempts to attract love.[11]

Yet 'Bardon Bus' and 'Accident' have much in common in their analyses of women's disposition towards shaping their lives as romantic fantasy plots – entertaining the same desires, suffering the same humiliations and then moving beyond the state of being in love back into a sense of self-possession at the end.

'Bardon Bus' is told by a woman alone, who is back in Toronto after a brief affair with a Canadian anthropologist in Australia a few months earlier. Her story combines both retrospective and present views of her emotional life, so that the reader has the constant impression of contradictory movement – of experience being lived through as well as being remembered – for in her telling, the narrator changes from being in love to resuming normal life again. She recovers, only to have her whole romance plot ironised through repetition as her friend Kay falls in love with the same man.

Organised on the 'centre and orbiting' principle, the story circles around the affair with X: 'I call him X, as if he were a character in an old-fashioned novel, that pretends to be true. X is a letter in his name' (*MJ*, 112). The narrator's particular predicament is situated within a long feminine tradition:

> Then I come back again and again to the center of my fantasy, to the moment when you give yourself up, give yourself over, to the assault which is guaranteed to finish off everything you've been before. (*MJ*, 111)

Such fantasies of self-surrender and transformation hint at parallels between the 'lifelong dream lives' of old unmarried aunts and the lives of modern women like the narrator and her friend Kay.

A remarkable feature of the story is its shifts in focus as the narrator remembers seemingly disparate episodes and anecdotes which did not seem significant at the time but which through hindsight seem to shape themselves into patterns of inevitability, like those links in the chain which Frances envisaged. Sections are related to one another by subjective processes of association so that hidden connections are brought to light, suggesting a deterministic structure while preserving the impression of randomness and unpredictability. Through the remembered fragments of Sir Walter Raleigh's poem written on the eve of his execution which are set beside memories of humiliating conversations with X's friend Dennis in Brisbane and Toronto about the role of biological determinism in women's lives, a barely repressed subtext of female dread is revealed. Stronger than the desire for love is this woman's fear of ageing and the loss of her powers of sexual attraction, which gives an urgency to this romantic fantasy script as well as the 'edgy sadness' which Munro commented upon.

Munro is fascinated by the extent to which women are willing to make spectacles of themselves in their attempts to create exciting scripts for their lives. It is that same impulse which connects the seemingly disparate Australian scenarios of passionate abandon in the 'golden twilight of love' with the darker autumnal scenario in a women's dress shop in Toronto later that same year: 'Thick sweaters and skirts are pinned up against black or plum-coloured velvet. The young salesgirls are made up like courtesans' (*MJ*, 124). As the narrator seeks feverishly for a 'more artful getup' we are reminded of Alicia Borinsky's comment on the relation between new clothes and women's fantasy lives:

> Store windows offer possibilities for the pose. They are for this woman alternative lives, a way to change. She does not buy clothes merely to be seen in them. As she puts on something new she gains access to a narrative where she is featured in a more intense plane.[12]

Such dressing up is only another form of masquerade as the narrator realises when 'the prettiest and most ladylike person I have seen all day' (*MJ*, 126) turns out to be a boy dressed up in women's clothes. It is a plotless, pointless performance ('What are you supposed to do now? Parade up and down on the sidewalk?') though no more pointless than her own, for the boy's question cuts straight through her disguise: 'How do I look, momma?'

That humiliating encounter signals a crucial stage in the narrator's recovery and later that afternoon, sitting alone in a Toronto coffee shop, she thinks for the first time of the pleasure of escaping from the trap of romance:

> When you start really letting go, this is what it's like ...
> It's an uncalled-for pleasure in seeing how the design
> wouldn't fit and the structure wouldn't stand, a pleasure
> in taking account, all over again, everything that is contra-
> dictory and persistent and unaccommodating about life.
> (*MJ*, 127–30)

Romantic fantasy comes to be distrusted finally because of what
it leaves out, for its flimsy configurations of desire fail to allow
for the ironies and contingencies of real life. Who would have
expected, for example, that the narrator's release from her
obsession with X would coincide with her friend Kay's falling in
love with him? That is what happens at the end of the story. Kay
confesses that she has fallen for 'Alex Walther, the anthropologist', and dressed up in a kinky 'new outfit, a dark-green
schoolgirl's tunic without a blouse or brassiere', she is ready to
begin the masquerade all over again (*MJ*, 128).

This emphasis on the 'innumerable repetitions, innumerable
variations' written into the scripts of individual lives is amplified
in the title story at the end which turns back to Janet Fleming's
family history, continuing the first story of the collection from a
different perspective. Here the cosmological imagery hinted at
earlier becomes explicit as the story makes a speculative attempt
to map patterns of significance on to changing circumstances. As
I have suggested, the satellite system of the Moons of Jupiter
provides an analogy for the design of the collection.[13] It also
provides a model of perpetual mobility on a scale so vast and so
complex that it marks the limits of human understanding at the
same time as it teases the mind into ever renewed efforts of
interpretation through the varied discourses of science and
poetry, religion, philosophy and myth. In this final story the
name of Jupiter the father of the gods is evoked with a particular
resonance for this is Janet Fleming's account of her father's last
illness. There are hints of a mythic pattern of correspondences
here, just as the story's structure confirms the 'centre and
orbiting' principle delineated earlier as the daughter's narrative
endlessly circles back through all its evasions and anxious
digressions to her father as he awaits a crucial heart operation.

As always, Munro's stories are located within a realistic frame of reference. Here it is Toronto, as Janet moves from the 'heart wing on the eighth floor of the Toronto General Hospital' to the planetarium beside the Royal Ontario Museum and then back again to her father's bedside. The story has a definite situation in place and time, yet the very word 'situation' when used by her father lying on his hospital bed (he keeps repeating the phrase 'in my situation') is a reminder that outside these narrow confines everything is uncertain. It is the prospect of imminent death which so disturbs the surface of this narrative as it moves restlessly between images of the wheeling heavens and the minutiae of bodily processes and human relationships. The father–daughter relationship is at the centre, though we are aware of a wider context as their conversations take place beside the indecipherable writing of his electrocardiograph and against Janet's report of her visit to the planetarium. These spectacular displays of the marvels and mysteries of science are an affront to the sensibilities of Janet and her father, for they are people bred up in long family traditions of reticence and self-sufficiency: 'I come of straitened people, madly secretive, tenacious, economical' (*MJ*, 10). As Janet says when she looks at the heart machine, 'The behaviour of his heart was on display. I tried to ignore it. It seemed to me that paying such close attention – in fact, drama-tizing what ought to be a most secret activity – was asking for trouble' (*MJ*, 217–18). Nevertheless, in a narrative characterised by its obliqueness, Munro does pay close attention to the most secret activities of human hearts – to the father's psychological preparations for death and to Janet's complex shifts of feeling as a daughter and as a mother, as she tries to come to terms with loss and bereavement.[14]

There are mysteries inside and outside, and it is in this context that the visit to the planetarium assumes its proper significance as the particularities of human experience are juxtaposed against the vast spectacle of the whirling cosmos. Such figuring of what is ungraspable and unknowable sets up powerful patterns of ambivalence here – between the father's recent attraction towards out-of-body experiences and a steady

refusal to be seduced by such visions of transcendence: 'Awe –
what was that supposed to be? A fit of the shivers when you
looked out the window? Once you knew what it was, you
wouldn't be courting it' (*MJ*, 232). Not the absence of awe but
the refusal to be unnerved by the awful, characterises the experience of both daughter and father here, for this is not a story
about spiritual revelations or a parable about divine order and
the presence of God.[15] On the contrary, it is insistently grounded
in the world of human affairs and confined to partial visions of
the mysteries which surround us. For all its high-tech impressive-
ness, the planetarium provides nothing more than an orchestrated
image of infinite space inside an enclosed dome, a paradox to
which the narrator draws attention when she tells her father
that it felt like being in 'a slightly phony temple' (*MJ*, 232).
James Carscallen remarks on 'the reflecting quality of Alice
Munro's revelations',[16] though I believe it is the artifice of
representation which is being highlighted here just as it was
with the electronic heart writing, for no model approaches the
dynamic complexity of reality: 'Whatever their purpose, maps
and models must simplify as much as they mimic the world.'[17]
From one point of view the spectacle of the heavens with their
'innumerable repetitions, innumerable variations' would seem
to have failed, and yet from another perspective it succeeds as
the dominant narrative image of transcendent patterning which
exceeds all human comprehension.

The story ends not with a gaze into the mysteries of the
cosmos but with a look at the world close at hand as Janet turns
back to rejoin her father in the hospital, when she will tell him
about her planetarium visit and they will discuss the Moons of
Jupiter in what will turn out to have been their last conversation
ever. There may be transcendental signifiers but there is no
Transcendental Signified available in this story. As her father
opines when speculating on the soul and the afterlife, 'Oh, I
don't know. It's all in whether you want to believe that kind of
thing or not' (*MJ*, 226). Revelation is not only constantly
deferred; it is also undesired.

In the last story, closure is refused as it has been in all the other stories; if anything, the dizzying shifts from known locations to the 'shoreless seas' of poetry and the 'horrible immensities' of science throw even more speculative possibilities into play. Yet within endless processes of change these stories do manage to construct images of provisional order, which centre on human relationships and connections – family connections, remembered connections, connections which may have been hidden, misunderstood or narrowly missed. These connections may be as unlikely as 'the way the stars tie up into their constellations' but nevertheless they are made through the performance of storytelling itself, where like the show in the planetarium, 'Realism is [was] abandoned, for familiar artifice' (*MJ*, 231).

The art of indeterminacy:
The Progress of Love

> The story circulates like a gift; an empty gift which
> anybody can lay claim to by filling it to taste, yet can
> never truly possess. A gift built on multiplicity. One that
> stays inexhaustible within its own limits. Its departures
> and arrivals. Its quietness.[1]

TRINH T. Minh-ha's image of women's oral storytelling in a
village marketplace suggests the process and method adopted by
Alice Munro in her sixth collection *The Progress of Love* (1986).
The analogy this time is not with cosmology or star maps but
with village gossip and its indirections in an approach where
'things are allowed to come forth, to grow wildly as "controlled
accidents" and to proceed in an unpredictable manner' so that
'one is compelled to look into the many facets of things and is
unable to point safely at them as if they were only outside
oneself.'[2] It is this emergence of story via digressions which
generate new meanings and resonances that is the distin-
guishing mark of *The Progress of Love*. The possible meanings
of a story are unsettled at every stage in the process of its telling,
so that every story in this collection is a series of disarrangements opening up spaces for new meanings. The
meaning of any story can never be determined either by the
narrator or by the reader; instead, Munro creates fictional
structures which allow for, indeed actively encourage, multiple
contradictory meanings and at the end leave a lot unaccounted
for. This is what I mean by her art of indeterminacy: her
narratives evade any single meaning but allow room for the

interplay of shifting multiple meanings and of multiple human interests.

As a theoretical concept, indeterminacy derives from Derridean *différance*, where attention is focused on the deferrals and instabilities of meaning inherent in language. My study also owes a debt to Michel Foucault's 'The Order of Discourse', to Trinh T. Minh-ha, and to Patricia McKie who has usefully explored indeterminacy in her version of poststructuralist literary theory.[3] Seeking to rehabilitate the status of human relations within the text and between the reader and the text (I would also add between the writer and the text), McKie emphasises parallels between the indeterminate relation of language to meaning and to human relations which are always evasive and excessive. Out of this concept a methodology might be developed for reading Munro's later stories where instability and irresolution characterise her narratives of human behaviour alone and in relationships. Perhaps the clearest way to introduce my discussion of indeterminacy in *The Progress of Love* is not via literary theory at all but via Munro's own analogy between a house and a short story, which I quote at the beginning of this book. It is significant that she does not talk about the objects in the house but about its rooms and about connections between the rooms:

> Everybody knows what a house does, how it encloses space and makes connections between one enclosed space and another and presents what is outside in a new way. This is the nearest I can come to explaining what a story does for me, and what I want my stories to do for other people.[4]

The three stories I have chosen, 'The Progress of Love', 'Fits' and 'White Dump' are all about houses and what they enclose and the connections made there through narrative, though there is always a space outside which resists the accommodation Munro's stories offer. What the stories enclose are spaces; they do not offer any single representation of meaning. The multiple stories within any one story may well be attempts to create meaning or they may merely repeat the remembered experience, but there are always gaps. The narrators are aware that language never quite connects with the experiences it evokes, and the reader is made aware by the spaces typographically signalled between different segments of the story that gaps leave room for more meanings than they formulate. In the shift from event to language, incalculable differences are introduced, because words do not coincide with events; stories have to be told by someone and as soon as there is a teller, that teller creates meanings which cannot be controlled or determined. This is the response of the narrator in 'The Progress of Love' to her mother's stories to her as a child: 'I always had a feeling, with my mother's talk and stories, of something swelling out behind. Like a cloud you couldn't see through, or get to the end of.'[5] This is not only a brilliant image for the floating signifier, but also an illustration of the way that Munro's stories encode a postmodern awareness of the strategies of fiction while at the same time deflecting the reader's attention away from such artifice through the domesticity of her language.

The stories in *Progress* make connections between experiences in the present and in the past, but they have no unifying plots which would establish causality or provide explicit relations between the parts of a narrative. Instead of depending on plots, her narratives depend on shifts from one point in time to another, from one point of view to another, covering and recovering the same ground from different angles. Such narratives do not annihilate differences or inconsistencies; they are full of disparities indicating different frames of reference – different interests of the tellers, different conditions of the telling – which render the truth indistinct and meaning indeterminate, like the direction of the story itself which is always shifting its ground. Its parts seem to go in multiple directions, so where is the structure? What kind of order is imposed in order to make the story possible? And what kind of satisfaction do we as readers get out of such stories? Is our pleasure similar to the narrator's in 'Bardon Bus', 'a pleasure in taking into account, all over again, everything that is contradictory and persistent and unaccommodating about life?' (*MJ*, 128). Yes it is, but for that narrator, pleasure depended on recognising the fragility of her romantic fantasy where 'the design wouldn't fit and the structure wouldn't stand', whereas Munro's narrative designs and structures do stand because they include those intractable elements of experience which romantic fantasy excludes. Her narrators have always revelled in incongruity and excess at the same time as they desire an impossible wholeness, like Del Jordan's wish for 'every last thing ... held still and held together, radiant, everlasting' (*LGW*, 249). Moments of radiance continue to be experienced by Munro's protagonists and her readers, but they have an increasingly provisional air about them, an illusory quality which culminates in the 'White Dump', that incongruous image of desire which is the title of the final story in this collection.

Though this chapter is concerned with three individual stories, the ironic juxtaposition of that last story with the title story at the beginning suggests that the principle of indeterminacy might be amplified by studying the arrangement of the collection as a whole. As was evident with *The Moons of Jupiter*, any one story reflects on and affects our reading of any other story within that collection, and their interrelationships make the reader aware that all the stories here are partial histories of love's progress. The very notion of a linear progress in love would seem to be subverted by these stories of male–female relationships over many years with their endless implications. Seeking a direction, the reader is thrown back to John Donne's 'Elegie XVIII: Love's Progress'[6] with its aggressively masculine declaration that progress can be measured in explicit terms of sexual conquest. However, even Donne has trouble in attaining 'The right true end of love', and as his poem develops it becomes a record of 'strayings' and 'errings', of shipwrecks and siren songs, and by the end the 'desired place' remains curiously unattainable. In this voyage of desire that never reaches its harbour the assertive male voice is forced to tell the story of a progress which is as inconclusive as anything in Munro. The difference is her feminine preference for indeterminacy over the determinations of progress and male mastery. Interestingly, she give the most extreme statement of this recognition to one of her male characters in the story 'Monsieur les Deux Chapeaux': 'Such progress seemed not only unnecessary but impossible. His life had split open, and nothing had to be figured out anymore' (*PL*, 82). Most of Munro's protagonists are, on the contrary, insistently figuring out their lives as she continues to figure out her stories, in a continuously shifting series of arrangements and rearrangements.

Every story is composed of segments of narrative (like the enclosed spaces in the house analogy) with time shifts between the segments, and these segments are often revisions of previous sections or additional fragments which seem only tangentially related. But these fragments are selected and their juxtaposition across the gaps indicates connections which are not spelled out but which the narrators believe in. These are the connections which Munro has always signalled, and we are reminded of an earlier story 'Winter Wind', when the narrator says:

> Yes, I have not invented it, I really believe it. Without any proof I believe it, and so I must believe that we get messages another way, that we have connections that cannot be investigated, but have to be relied on. (*SIBM*, 161)

The narrator in 'The Progress of Love' is saying much the same thing when she discovers that a story she believes to be true is one which she has actually invented: 'How hard it is for me to believe that I made that up. It seems so much the truth it is the truth; it's what I believe about them' (*PL*, 30). For Munro there is always the irony of belief which coincides with an inability to know, though the absence of knowledge does not preclude belief. These connections do not resolve anything; they merely keep different often contradictory meanings in circulation. Yet these fictional houses do not collapse; they retain their realistic framework but they also recognise that there is a great deal that cannot be accommodated, that remains outside, 'floating around loose, ignored but powerful' like death in 'Heirs of the Living Body' (*LGW*, 46). The endings of these stories are not closures but they give significance to what has gone before, allowing us to see what is outside – and inside – the story in a new way.

It is worth looking into the narrative consequences of this art of indeterminacy: 'The Progress of Love' and 'White Dump' are concerned with an excess of stories that linger in the protagonists' memories but which do not illuminate anything for them, while 'Fits' is concerned with a crucial refusal to tell the true story of what really happened. In 'The Progress of Love' the storytelling process is activated by her father's phone call to a woman called Phemie (the narrator) to say that her mother has died, and the story consists of Phemie's memories of her mother and in turn her own mother's stories about her mother. What Phemie would like to do is to make these enigmas fit into her own story about herself and what she has become as an adult, a divorced mother of two sons who works in a real estate office in the small town not far from the farm where she was brought up. She retells her mother's and grandmother's stories, shifting back into the past: her mother's story about her childhood when she found *her* mother out in the barn threatening to hang herself because she believed her husband was having an affair with someone: 'Her heart was broken. That was what I always heard my mother say. That was the end of it' (PL, 13). But of course it was not the end for anybody; for Phemie's mother it induced a poison of hatred for her father which caused her first of all to become religious and then years later to burn the three thousand dollars which he left to her in his will, even though that meant depriving her daughter of a college education.

The events of Phemie's story are loosely structured around the farmhouse where she grew up: memories of repapering a room when she was twelve for the visit of her mother's sister Aunt Beryl from California, and Phemie's return years later to that same house with a male friend called Bob Marks after her parents had died and the house had had several different owners. On both occasions it is the story of her mother's burning of her inheritance which is foregrounded. We are given two completely different versions of it and two different judgements. The way Phemie tells it to Bob Marks is that her father watched her mother burning the money and did not try to stop her, and Phemie sees that as a kind of love. When Marks says that some people would consider it lunacy, Phemie remembers, 'that had been Beryl's opinion, exactly' (*PL*, 26). Beryl's version of their childhood contradicted Phemie's mother's and Beryl's version did not vanish: 'It stayed sealed off for years, but it was not gone' (*PL*, 23). Phemie recalls that it was actually in Beryl's company that her mother revealed that she had burned the money and that she had done it alone; Phemie's father had not been there at all. What Phemie wonders at the end is how she got her belief in that story of her parents' love when she knows it is not true. And why does she let Bob Marks believe a comforting lie at the end? She tells us it is because she thinks that in modern relationships where everything is temporary that 'moments of kindness and reconciliation are worth having, even if the parting has to come sooner or later' (*PL*, 30).

The story takes so long to tell because there is no plot line which can be summarised, and Phemie's mother's and grand-mother's stories have so many drifting meanings which cannot be repressed or made sense of, let alone contained. They remain resistant to the urge to shape them into any kind of explanation of the woman Phemie has herself become or to offer any con-firmation of her role as family chronicler. Is this a story about love, as Phemie wants to be? Or is it a story about hatred, that clot of poison that stains a life 'like a drop of black ink in white milk' (*PL*, 6)? Certainly her mother's and grandmother's stories are about hatred and unforgivable acts, and I wonder if Phemie's retelling them after her mother's death is not an expression of her own inability to forgive her mother, as well as her attempt to forgive her? When she ends the story by talking about those old marriages like her parents' 'where love and grudges could be growing underground, so confused and stubborn, it must have seemed they had forever' (*PL*, 31), is she not implicated in her parents' story and in the social consequences of her mother's act, where the love and the grudges are hers too? So there is another sense in which the meaning of these stories is indeterminate: they do not end but go on circulating in the memory of the narrator, 'the stories, and griefs, the old puzzles you can't resist or solve' (PL, 14).

There is no clear distinction between what is real and what is fictional, just as there is no clear boundary between knowledge and belief. The meaning of these stories is never independent of the teller's interpretation. It is not a question of the lack of meaning but of multiple meanings 'growing underground, confused and stubborn' which negate any notion of progress, and call into question the difference between hatred and love. Phemie's predicament is the same as the narrator's in 'The Ottawa Valley':

> The problem, the only problem, is my mother. And she is the one of course that I am trying to get: it is to reach her that this whole journey has been undertaken. With what purpose? To mark her off, to describe, to illumine, to celebrate, to *get rid* of her; and it did not work. (*SIBM*, 235)

It is interesting that forgiveness or the hope of it comes only much later in another story in this collection where in 'Miles City, Montana' a mother trusts that some time in the future she and her husband will be forgiven by their daughters for 'all our natural, and particular, mistakes' (PL, 105).

'Fits' can be treated more economically for it does not have the same kind of redundancy as 'Progress'. Indeed it is quite sharply focused for a Munro story, but again there are no explanations. It is about a murder–suicide in the small town of Gilmore which is discovered by Peg Kuiper, the woman who lives next door. Typically for Munro, realistic detail and ordinariness are highlighted and the extraordinary event is introduced obliquely in amongst neighbourly gestures and egg deliveries in snowy weather. The opening sentence of the story is: 'The two people who died were in their early sixties' (PL, 106), and there follows a brief account of Mr and Mrs Weeble having drinks on Boxing Day with Peg and Robert Kuiper and Peg's two teenage sons. Then the focus shifts away from the Weebles entirely to Peg and Robert and their life together, and readers are told how Peg's first husband, a truck driver, had driven trucks further and further away till he ended up in the Arctic.

The story of the Weebles' murder–suicide is told with lots of gaps and shifts between different people's points of view. The first version given is Robert's reconstruction: 'He pictured what happened' (*PL*, 111) from the reports of the only two eye witnesses of the aftermath of the catastrophe: Peg's, for it was she who found the bodies when she went over to deliver the eggs before going to work, and the local constable's, from whom Robert first heard the story in a highway diner later that day. Robert was not there as he was away from Gilmore on a job. What his version and everyone else's versions reveal are their limits of knowledge. Peg is very restrained and she restricts herself to giving the bare facts: 'Yes. I found them … It was a murder–suicide … He shot her and then he shot himself. That's what happened' (*PL*, 116). Indeed these are the only facts, and the rest of the story interweaves the multiple explanations people offer in order to try to accommodate this extraordinary happening, phoning each other, 'just … anybody they could think of who might not have heard' (*PL*, 118), trying from hearsay to determine the events and their cause. Of course all the explanations are 'equally plausible … equally hollow and useless' (*PL*, 119) and it is only Peg who insists that *nobody* knows what happened.

When Robert suggests at dinner that evening that perhaps the murder–suicide was a freak thing like a volcano or an earthquake, 'a kind of fit', one of Peg's sons remarks that an earthquake is not a freak though maybe it could called 'a periodic fit' (*PL*, 126) and he reminds his mother of the fights which she and her first husband used to have. Suddenly Robert sees on his wife's face an expression of 'helpless, unapologetic pain', which causes him in turn remember a fight he once had with a former girlfriend, something he wants 'absolutely and eternally … to forget about' (*PL*, 128). Of course, like Beryl's stories, such things may be sealed over for years but they are still there.

That night when Robert goes out alone walking in the snow he is turning over in his mind one crucial detail he had been meaning to ask Peg about. In her account to him of what she saw, she said she knew something was terribly wrong because she saw one of Mr Weeble's legs lying in the passage at the top of the stairs. But Robert is baffled by 'one discrepancy, one detail – one lie – that would never have anything to do with him' (*PL*, 130). Then as he walks on, he sees something very odd, a great glittering mass under the trees:

> A congestion of shapes, with black holes in them, and unmatched arms or petals reaching up to the lower branches of the trees. He headed toward these shapes, but whatever they were did not become clear. They did not look like anything he knew. (*PL*, 130)

This is the one piece of promising-looking figurative language in the story and it functions as a kind of epiphany; or it could have been so in a modernist short story, an image for the lie at the centre of Peg's version or for the elusiveness of meaning in the murder–suicide. However Munro does not tell it as epiphany, focusing meaning; instead she does just the opposite. Of course there are possible connections which might be made between the 'black holes' and Peg's lie and the deep well in Yucatan that the Weebles had mentioned on their Boxing Day visit, but there is a lot more to that mass than holes. Indeed, a speculative essay might be written on the importance of rubbish heaps in Munro's stories, which sit alongside her well-ordered lists. These heaps have very little if any meaning in a literal sense, but they are presented as jumbles of signifiers whose appearance is usually deceptive. On closer examination Robert sees that the mysterious glittering monstrosities in the snow are only old cars and that the black holes are their gutted insides. He thinks of telling Peg 'how close he had to get before he saw that what amazed him and bewildered him so was nothing but old wrecks' and how he felt both disappointed and like laughing and finally 'more like going home' (*PL*, 131). The idea of wreckage within is most significant here, and the fact that the 'old wrecks' no longer looked like 'anything he knew' does not deny the fact that they were only useless old cars. Robert insists that he just had to get very 'close' (that word occurs three times in two paragraphs) before he could see into the monstrous twisted shapes.[7]

The story ends on the revelation of the one discrepant detail in Peg's story to Robert, highlighted by the version which the constable had told him. It was Walter Weeble's shot-off head ('What was left of it') that was lying out in the hall, not the leg as Peg had said. In the last paragraph Robert contemplates the possible implications of Peg's omission:

> Not a leg ... whole and decent in its trousers, the shod foot. That was not what anybody turning at the top of the stairs would see and would have to step over, step through, in order to go into the bedroom and look at the rest of what was there. (*PL*, 131)

The enclosed spaces and the black holes remain. Though connections can be made in narratives and in human relationships, they are always made across gaps and secrets and they are always provisional and incomplete. All this returns us to the house analogy with a difference: these stories allow us to see not only what is outside in a new way but also what is inside. In addition they also point to the virtues of indeterminacy and the necessity for secrets as they hint at what one 'would have to step over, step through, in order to look at the rest of what was there' (*PL*, 131).

'White Dump' is a house story too, though the house has undergone extensive renovations over a period of fifteen years which is the time the story occupies in its chronicle of the breakup of a marriage and its aftermath. It is divided into three numbered sections, each signalling the points of view and attendant limits of vision of one of the three female protagonists: Denise the daughter, Sophie the grandmother, and Isabel the mother. Again, shifts in time and narrative perspective preclude any single interpretation and no authoritative value judgement is imposed on the feelings and events recounted. The White Dump of the title occurs only once, told as an anecdote by the mother towards the end. The narrative itself looks like an assemblage of fragments but is it, like the heap of scarves lying on an old chest in the redecorated house, really a '*calculated* jumble' (*PL*, 276), a triumph of artifice? Certainly there are obvious connections between the three parts: family relationships, the house by the lake, the overlapping events which are told and retold from different angles. These form the basic structure of this house of fiction; but Munro's narrative artifice lies elsewhere, in the hidden connections which she figures out between the 'enclosed spaces' the story contains while at the same time she builds in her recognition of the duplicities and secrets within any fictive construct.

The recurring points of reference in this decentred narrative are the fortieth birthday celebrations of Laurence (the father–son–husband figure) and the special treat that his daughter arranged for him. Turning to his second wife, Laurence asks, 'Magda, did you know that on my fortieth birthday Denise took me up in a plane?' (*PL*, 278) What neither Denise nor her father mentions is that this was also the day of Isabel's meeting with the pilot and the beginning of the affair that put an end 'to her marriage, though not to his' (*PL*, 308). As an adult visitor to the house, Denise contemplates its present 'layers of harmony and satisfaction' (*PL*, 288) together with her layers of memory beneath, recalling not only the birthday flight but also another visitor, the pilot's wife who burst into tears in that same room where she is now standing. Denise's story is marked by 'signs of pain' – the woman's 'spurts of sound' (*PL*, 287), the pilot's strange tale of St Elmo's Fire when blue flames spurted from his fingertips, and of course her own pain at her mother's inexplicable behaviour. Like Phemie in 'Progress' Denise is haunted by the 'old puzzles you can't resist or solve' (*PL*, 14).

The point of view shifts radically in the second section, where 'Sophie's tread made the floorboards shudder' (*PL*, 289). Known in her family as 'Old Norse' because she was an Assistant Professor of Scandinavian Languages and because of her fierce unconventionality, Sophie's experiences on her son's birthday open out to dimensions of violence not present in the rest of the narrative. These culminate in her intuitions of disaster on the birthday flight as she looks down at the hidden rocks beneath the calm surface of the lake:

> Her feeling of a mistake, of a very queer and incom-
> municable problem, did not abate. It wasn't the approach
> but the aftermath of disaster she felt, in this golden air – as
> if they were all whisked off and cancelled, curled up into
> dots, turned to atoms, but they didn't know it. (*PL*, 296)

Such strangeness cannot be accommodated within the discourse of family life, so Sophie must remain silent – as does Isabel in the third section, though for different reasons.

Isabel's section is preoccupied with a wife's version of the birthday, involving the domestic hurdles to be overcome in order to make it a success. She is the one who waits quietly on the ground when the family go up in the plane, and the pilot's invitation to her to go for a flight alone with him is presented as an unlikely interruption of her daily routine and closer to fantasy than to real life. Certainly Isabel's anecdote that night about the White Dump of her schooldays belongs to the realm of fantasy too. This is another of Munro's duplicitous rubbish heaps (made this time from the sweepings of the local biscuit factory floor), an image of desire so powerful that it overcomes prudence, just as Isabel's affair with the pilot will do. There is a shift towards the end (but no typographical break) to the older divorced Isabel's words to her grown-up daughter when she speaks about sexual desire in language strikingly similar to the description of the White Dump.

The story retires back into the domestic framework of the birthday, though it does not end there. Instead, there is a final shift in the frame of reference to a two-line quotation from *The Poetic Edda* which Sophie has left on her chair last thing that night and which Isabel reads:

> *Seinat er at segia;*
> *svá er nu rádit.*
> (It is too late to talk of this now: it has been decided.)
> (*PL*, 309)

These verses come from the twelfth-century Old Icelandic saga, 'Atlamal in Groenlenzko' which is a story of invitation, betrayal and revenge, pervaded by women's warning dreams, runic messages and an overpowering sense of fate.[8] They offer a deterministic reading of events which chimes with Sophie's intuitions but which refers to an ancient form of discourse at odds with the apparent randomness and multiple perspectives of Munro's narrative. It is tempting to seek a parallel between her 'calculated jumble' and the defaced runic message of the Atlamal poem (not quoted by Munro):

> The runes were so confused / she could hardly construe them.[9]

Are Isabel's actions already scripted beyond her own knowledge, or is that Atlamal poem another example of a narrative whose 'horrible plausible connections' Munro's stories claim to reject? This story entertains both possibilities, implicating the reader in an attempt to construe meanings that remain tantalisingly open to reinterpretation.

There is another kind of indeterminacy which lies behind the published text and which relates to the creative process, as can be seen in Munro's manuscript drafts of her stories. Examining the drafts in the University of Calgary Library of the three stories discussed here, I discovered some interesting continuities and variations between versions.[10] The main blocks of narrative remain constant, as if certain incidents are put into circulation early in the storytelling process though these blocks are then rearranged and fractured by the introduction of time-shifts and different narrative perspectives; they are shifted about until an apparently appropriate ordering is arrived at. (Looking at the drafts, one can imagine a different ordering of these blocks which would then have made a different narrative configuration. The story elements are there, but Munro's constant rearrangements suggest multiple possibilities of signification.) A few examples must suffice here to demonstrate Munro's treatment of the 'inexhaustible empty gift' of the story. In 'Progress' changes in narrative perspective are the most notable feature. In the typescript for *The New Yorker* version (published October 7, 1985) Phemie's first-person narrative is changed to the third person throughout, and similar oscillations occur in other undated fragments though consistency is maintained within any particular version.[11] With 'Fits' the major changes are in the direction of narrative economy and suspense, where the drafts all fill in the blank of what Peg reported on the murder–suicide at least two pages before it is revealed in the published version.[12] All versions, however, keep the revelation of the leg/head discrepancy till the end.

The evolution of 'White Dump' is more fully chronicled than the other two, with multiple drafts and fragments available, beginning with a holograph version in a red notebook titled 'St Elmo's Fire'.[13] The rearrangements and gradual emergence of the final version may be plainly seen, and the early possibility of a deterministic principle hovers in the notebook version where astrology and horoscopes are foregrounded. There is a great deal of rewriting of the segment about Isabel's meeting with the pilot and the forms of romantic fantasy within which this infidelity is encoded, and there are two versions which are more explicit about her behaviour on the birthday evening. They both suggest a principle of determinism, but one which is psychological rather than supernatural like *The Poetic Edda* (cf. published version, *PL*, 306–7): Version (a):

> All that evening, under her attention to the meal, to the conversation, an attention more whole-hearted, lively than usual, Susan [Isabel] had the same picture in her mind. It was of herself doing something that was unlikely, absurd, and terrifying, yet it was as clear as a memory, as unavoidable as if she had already done it.[14]

and Version (b):

> So now on the evening of Bryan's [Laurence's] birthday she knows – but, still guiltless, doesn't know. She doesn't know for sure that she will find herself, tomorrow morning, walking across that grass and gravel towards that building, nothing yet declared, nothing transformed.[15]

The drafts show Munro experimenting with the different kinds of significance that events may assume when they are put together in different orders, as if events in themselves have undecodable meanings and can only be taken account of by being fitted into a narrative framework constructed by the storytellers (who include, of course, Munro herself). The story does have authority for the very fact of its existence is a figuring of limits, a structure (to return to the house analogy), the result as the drafts reveal of arrangements and renovations which impose a narrative order by 'relating' events, in both senses of that word. Munro creates a discontinuous discourse riddled with signs of incompleteness which is designed to accommodate the disorder of multiple interpretations, and her narratives themselves offer models for such misreadings/misrecognitions.

In these stories Munro comes close to Trinh T. Minh-ha's plurality of meaning which 'radiates from language, whose fictional nature is precisely what tends to be denied in every attempt to subject it to the ideological norms of clarity and accessibility.'[16] In the writing of both these women there is always excess and incompleteness, a resistance to closure and classification. Indeterminacy has become the principle within narrative structures as within human relationships:

> If I had been younger, I would have figured out a story …
> I would have made a horrible, plausible connection
> between that silence of his, and the manner of his death.
> Now I no longer believe that people's secrets are defined
> and communicable, or their feelings full-blown and easy
> to recognize. I don't believe so (MJ, 35).

On lies, secrets, and silence:
Friend of My Youth

Re-vision – the act of looking back, of seeing with fresh
eyes, of entering an old text from a new critical direction –
is for women more than a chapter in cultural history: it is
an act of survival.[1]

THE stories in *Friend of My Youth* (1990) are constantly
engaged with looking back – into personal and family history,
into Canadian colonial history and the Scots–Canadian cultural
inheritance – though like Adrienne Rich's purposeful re-
visioning echoed in this chapter title and initial quotation, these
are not exercises in sentimental nostalgia but attempts to
discover new significance in the present by making connections
with the past. These stories are long and complex, for 'strange
bits of the world get into Munro's stories: digressions of every
sort, family histories, notes on cultural artefacts ... newspaper
articles, old letters, and very often, seemingly random anecdotes
beaded on a thin string of narrative'.[2] Both Munro and Rich are
writing against the erasure of women's history and the
suppression of women's voices through 'the lies and distortions
of the culture that men have devised'.[3] However, Munro's
intricate explorations uncover lies, self-deceptions and hidden
imperatives within the stories that women too have devised for
their lives just as her increasingly self-conscious narrators
realise the inevitability of distortion within the storytelling
process itself. *On Lies, Secrets, and Silence* would have been an
appropriate title for this collection, as in the three stories I have
chosen to discuss evasion and secrecy are the common

denominators. All three are stories about women who manage to elude the conventional plots of their own lives: the mother in 'Friend of My Youth' whose story has already been scripted by her daughter and by her own illness; the nineteenth-century woman poet in 'Meneseteung' who escapes colonial social expectations by retreating into eccentricity; and the middle-aged wife in 'Oranges and Apples' who refuses to play out her designated role in her husband's melodramatic plots of infidelity and disaster.

The title story in this collection dedicated by Munro to the memory of her mother is a re-vision of that ongoing auto-biographical narrative which critics have described as the ground base of her art: 'The writing daughter's conscious failure to understand or represent the mother remains at the heart of Alice Munro's aesthetic.'[4] Told in the first-person confessional form, it is a daughter's story about the mother who will not go away but even after death seems to go on living and changing in the underworld of her daughter's dream life. But that is only the frame story, for embedded within it is the Ontario Gothic tale told by that mother about the Grieves sisters and their story of love and betrayal, which in its turn is added to over the years by pieces of supplementary information through letters exchanged, then later rewritten not twice but three times by the dying mother and her daughter – once during the mother's lifetime and again after her death. Not only does the story circulate as gossip in proliferating versions but it is also the topic of an ongoing dialogue between daughter and absent mother and subjected to several radical reinterpretations, up to the point where the daughter can no longer distinguish between pro-tagonists and tellers. This leads to her final recognition that 'of course it's my mother I'm thinking of' and her somewhat startling revelation at the end.[5] If it is a story about women's storytelling, it is perhaps more explicitly a story about women's writing, for the daughter's narrative includes her mother's and her friends' letters to one another (indeed it is named after a phrase of greeting from one of her mother's unfinished letters) and it is also includes her mother's unwritten novel about the

Grieves sisters and her own subsequent revisions. The story extends over many years, from the mother's early days to her death, stretching forward into the narrator's present and backward at the very end to the seventeenth century and into another country with its historical anecdote about the Scottish Covenanters who were the ancestors of the Grieves family in twentieth-century Ontario.

Even telling the bare outlines of this story generates the kind of frustration experienced by another of Munro's narrators in another story in this book, 'Differently':

> Georgia once took a creative-writing course, and what the instructor told her was: Too many things. Too many things going on at the same time; also too many people. Think, he told her. What is the important thing? What do you want us to pay attention to? Think. (*FMY*, 216)

A possible way through the densely interwoven network is to focus on the daughter's opening dream, to see how it relates to the stories about Flora Grieves and also the reason why the daughter cannot let Flora's story alone: 'I used to dream about my mother, and though the details in the dream varied, the surprise in it was always the same' (*FMY*, 3). In that dream her mother is alive and quite well, as if she has shed her paralysing disease and lightly forgives the daughter for neglecting her so long. That dream, so 'transparent in its hopefulness', is abandoned for the story of Flora Grieves on her Ottawa Valley farm and how she survived the double betrayal by her fiancé Robert Deal, who married her younger sister Ellie after having made her pregnant, and then when Ellie died of cancer married not Flora but Ellie's nurse. It is that unfinished story with its opacity and its endless supplements which seems to focus our attention just as it obsesses mother and daughter, who offer different versions of it at different times. The mother tells it later in her life as 'The Maiden Lady', the story of a high-minded religious woman (for the Grieveses belonged to an extreme Calvinist sect called the Cameronians).[6] The daughter opposes her mother's views and systems of value by telling it as the

story of a 'black Presbyterian witch' who is finally defeated by
the nurse, complete with a book-burning and the eradication of
that 'monstrous old religion' (*FMY*, 13) which Flora had
believed in. Yet that story continues to surface for there is
always a sequel – first in Flora's own letter to the dying mother
to say that she has left the farm and gone to work in town in a
shop, and then in the daughter's later imagining of what she
would say if she ever met Flora. She tells that version after the
deaths of her mother and Flora when she feels free to invent, and
of course she knows that this is a daydream – which returns her
by a kind of circular movement to the dream of her mother at
the beginning. Despite its apparent circularity, the plot has
moved on and discoveries have been made. As she contemplates
the imagined Flora's gently mocking silence, she realises that
she has been transposing Flora and her mother and that both of
these figures have eluded her. She is outside their stories and of
course none of the letters was addressed to her; moreover, her
mother's unfinished letters were the sick woman's pathetic
attempts to reach out beyond her loneliness through the comforting fiction of social intercourse denied her by her daughter.
We may remember what another of Munro's protagonists says
about the underground life of dreams in the next story, 'Five
Points':

> This system is not like roads or tunnels but more like a live
> body network, all coiling and stretching, unpredictable but
> finally familiar – where you are now, where you've
> always been. (*FMY*, 37)

However, the most subversive aspect of her earlier dream is not
her mother's disconcertingly good health but the shadowy feeling
behind her own relief at this recovery. The daughter realises
that she needs her mother to stay sick in order to maintain a
sense of her own identity as daughter and writer, and that she
does not wish to revise that old text of the tormented relationship with her mother:

> I would have to say that I felt slightly cheated. Yes,
> offended, tricked, cheated, by this welcome turnaround,

> this reprieve. My mother moving rather carelessly out of
> her old prison, showing options and powers I never
> dreamed she had, changes more than herself. (*FMY*, 26)

This is a difficult, not to say unspeakable, revelation only to be
approached indirectly through those multiple re-visions of
Flora's story. And what of the final anecdote about the
Cameronians, returning to a violent pre-Canadian past with
tales of religious murder and hangings and excommunications?
Though it obviously relates to Flora's religion, is her mother not
implicated once again in this story about Flora's ancestors?
Carol Shields suggests that this is the story's final statement
about the absolute integrity of the self: 'To be understood,
Munro suggests in the radiant, divergent final paragraph, is to be
invaded and colonised; hanging on to your own life may mean the
excommunication of *all* others.'[7] There is no patriarchal ranting
in this story but a steadfast rejection of coercion by these two
women (the mother and Flora) who preserve their integrity
through stratagems of secrecy and silence.

'Meneseteung' presents Munro's contribution to the
feminist re-visionary project of reconstructing a female literary
tradition by recovering the work of forgotten women writers.
As Canadian critic Carole Gerson remarks in her essay on the
disappearance of so many nineteenth-century Canadian women
poets' names from twentieth-century anthologies,

> Tired of being cheated of recognition by the literary
> establishment, the early Canadian woman poet has deviously
> begun to re-enter our literature in fictional form, in Carol
> Shields' *Mary Swann: A Mystery* and Alice Munro's
> 'Meneseteung'.[8]

Munro's story about a fictive nineteenth-century woman poet
who lived in the small town of Goderich in southwestern
Ontario pays attention to issues highlighted by feminist critics,
such as social assumptions about femininity, women's domestic
roles as daughters, wives and mothers, and also to the dualities
experienced by women artists whose creative powers conflicted
with conventional feminine expectations. The American critic

Mary Poovey's study of eighteenth-century literary women *The Proper Lady and the Woman Writer* provides the focus for my discussion of Munro's exploration of that double role and its disruptive effects on a woman's life,[9] so that her story becomes a critique of nineteenth-century Canadian colonial society and its attitudes to women and to 'poetesses' in particular. Yet precisely because it is a fiction and not a piece of literary criticism Munro is free to invent her character's life story, combining psychobiography with local history of place as well as a recognition of her own role as narrator. She is also free to highlight those topics which interest her most: the traditional Canadian trope of women and wilderness, issues of gender, sexuality and female bodies, and crucially women's pleasure in writing – be it history, fiction or poetry.

This story has an apparently decorous old-fashioned structure, beginning with a scrupulous account of the (fictive) historical evidence available, as the narrator describes the book of poems which she finds:

> *Offerings* the book is called. Gold lettering on a dull-blue cover. The author's full name underneath: Almeda Joynt Roth. The local paper, the *Vidette*, referred to her as 'our poetess.' (*FMY*, 50)

The book, published 1873, has the author's photo as frontispiece as well as a preface giving details of her life. The photo is described in detail, as are a selection of her poems, stanzas of which are used to introduce each of the six sections into which the story is divided. Almeda's life and her poetry would seem to conform to colonial constructions of middle-class femininity with her family's pioneer history, her role as unmarried house-keeper for her widowed father, and her poems on conventional Victorian subjects like childhood, death and landscape; as Munro says, they are 'poems about birds and wild flowers and snowstorms' (*FMY*, 52).

Yet there are striking oddities here: first the mysterious title of the story, and then Almeda's ambiguous challenge to gender construction in her portrait where she looks like 'a young nobleman of another century' as well as her fascination with heroic exploration narratives in a poem called 'Champlain at the Mouth of the Meneseteung'. (This is where we realise that the story's title is the ancient Indian name for the Maitland River, at the mouth of which Goderich is situated.)

Munro foregrounds the documentary evidence for her historical reconstruction, where in addition to the book of poems she refers to old photographs of the town and to reports in the local newspaper. (Curiously, the *Vidette* was the name of the local paper in Munro's home town of Wingham in 1883, though the name of the Goderich paper in this period was the *Signal Star*.) She pays attention to the town's economic and material development in the late nineteenth-century with the coming of the railway, local industries, sawmills and brickyards – all typical features of raw new towns built on the edge of the Canadian wilderness. The *Vidette* also supplies a skeleton outline of Almeda's life story after the publication of her single volume: her prospects of marriage to the respectable citizen and Civil Magistrate, Jarvis Poulter, followed by a brief news item on her discovery of a drunken woman's body near the back of her house, and then a gap of over twenty years till the notices of Almeda's death in 1903 and of Jarvis Poulter's in 1904. Apparently they never married. Munro's narrative effort is dedicated to filling in these gaps and to constructing a logic behind scraps of newspaper gossip. Only the first and last sections are set in the present, so forming a frame for the imaginative reconstruction of a woman's relation to place and to poetry, for this is the story of Almeda's transformations from sentimental poetess into romantic wilderness visionary and town eccentric.

Munro's story is a playful mixture of fact and fiction, an imaginative re-visioning of history. Just as Goderich is not named though easily identifiable from its situation on Lake Huron and its salt wells discovered in 1866, so I believe that Almeda is 'partly real' rather than 'wholly invented', as Claire Tomalin speculated in her review of *Friend of My Youth*.[10] I would suggest that Almeda's shadowy parallel may be found in the forgotten nineteenth-century poet Eloise A. Skimings

(1836–1921), a native of Goderich and known locally as 'the poetess of Lake Huron'. Her photo appears in the Huron County Museum in Goderich as it does on the frontispiece to her one book of poems, *Golden Leaves*, published by Signal Press, Goderich, in 1904. Like Almeda's *Offerings*, the book also has a pale-blue cover with gold lettering on it. Her poems, many of them addressed to persons who had presented her with flowers (like 'a double golden petaled tulip' or 'gold and crimson water lilies') are full of Victorian sentimentality, though one of them is about 'the proud Maitland River' and another 'Reminiscence of Early Days' begins remarkably enough with the phrase 'friend of my youth' in its first line:

> Friend of my infancy, friend of my youth,
> > Thou are just the same to me
> As when we roamed adown the glassy slopes
> > Of old Huron's rippling sea.
>
> > > > *(Golden Leaves*, p. 6)

Skimings (known in her family as the diminutive 'Eliza') was unmarried too, though looking through her letters I could find no trace of a Jarvis Poulter figure. Indeed, their 'life stories' would appear to have been different, though both are buried in Goderich cemetery. However, these sketchy similarities grounded in local history provide fascinating glimpses into Munro's fictional transformations of real material.[11]

Almeda's story conforms to nineteenth-century convention with its descriptions of traditional feminine occupations and domestic spaces. However, her house has a double view for though its frontage is on the respectable main street, its back windows overlook a very poor quarter and a patch of undrained bogland, the Pearl Street Swamp. The wilderness is still there on the edge, and Pearl Steet with its drunken disorder and violence marks the borderline of settlement beyond which glimmers the pristine wilderness. Almeda can see it like a mirage from her bedroom window:

> She can see the sun rising, the swamp mist filling with
> light, the bulky, nearest trees floating against that mist

and the trees behind turning transparent. Swamp oaks,
soft maples, tamarack, bitternut. (*FMY*, 56)

Almeda Roth in her late thirties is still encased in her
Victorian image of the 'proper lady', and her romantic aspirations are restricted to thoughts of marriage with Jarvis Poulter.
Wanting a hero, she believes that he with his uncompromising
masculinity would fulfil her desires:

> She wants a man who doesn't have to be made, who is firm
> already and determined and mysterious to her. She does
> not look for companionship. (*FMY*, 60)

Yet even as she decorously fantasises marriage and dreams of
the public trappings of courtship like a drive with him into the
country, a note of ambivalence creeps in for she knows that this
relationship would interfere with her imaginative life and her
labours of poetic composition: 'Glad to be beside him ... And
sorry to have the countryside removed for her – filmed over, in
a way, by his talk and preoccupations' (*FMY*, 61). Almeda's
landscape poetry (as we can tell from the quoted passages) is
sentimental fabrication and highly selective of its raw materials;
the countryside that she has written about actually takes
'diligence and determination to see'. In the way she measures
loss as well as gain in her romantic fantasy we have a hint of
Almeda's 'shy and stubborn eccentricity' which cannot easily be
accommodated within conventional femininity.

This delicately nurtured feminine world is split apart by the
incident of the drunken brawl and the woman's body against her
back fence reported in the *Vidette*. For once, violence and carnal-
ity intrude into Almeda's consciousness on a hot summer night:

> It's as if there were a ball of fire rolling up Pearl Street,
> shooting off sparks ... yells and laughter and shrieks and
> curses, and the sparks are voices that shoot off alone
> (*FMY*, 63).

Almeda hears confused sounds of a man and a woman fighting,
followed by 'a long, vibrating, choking sound of pain and self-
abasement, self-abandonment' which in her innocence she

interprets as murder but which are really the sounds of sex. When next morning Almeda goes out and finds the woman's body still there, she is so upset by the sight that she runs barefoot in her nightgown to ask for Jarvis Poulter's help. In his worldly wisdom he takes one look at the body, prods the bare bruised leg 'as you'd nudge a dog or a sow' (FMY, 66) and shoos the woman home like an animal, rather coarsely remarking, 'There goes your dead body' (FMY, 67). Though Almeda feels sick enough to retch, seeing this female body and how it is treated by men (including Jarvis Poulter) she suddenly becomes aware of her own sexuality through an odd sympathetic connection below the level of consciousness, just as paradoxically Poulter becomes aware of Almeda's sexuality as well. Now he makes the declaration which is tantamount to a marriage proposal: 'I will walk with you to church' – and she refuses him.

Her body becomes the site of resistance, and returning home she finds that she has begun to menstruate, so she locks herself inside her house and ignores Jarvis Poulter's knock at the door. Instead, she takes a dose of her nerve medicine (probably based on laudanum) with a cup of tea and spends the day in 'perfect immobility' sitting enclosed in her overdecorated colonial dining room. The only sound she can hear is the 'plop, plop' of the grape juice falling from its swollen purple cheesecloth bag into a basin beneath, for she had started to make some grape jelly the evening before. This is Almeda's crisis, possibly diagnosable as a minor nervous breakdown though also possibly as a sign of her strange liberation – for through that state of drug-induced hypersensitivity Almeda finds access to her poetic imagination once more where 'Everything seems charged with life, ready to move and flow and alter. Or possibly to explode' (FMY, 69). She begins to conceive a new poem which will 'contain everything', with all her former sentimental subjects supplemented by 'the obscene racket on Pearl Street' and the woman's body, as she makes the leap beyond sentimentality into a new world of imaginative excess where everything overflows and merges – history and prehistory, domestic details, her own unspeakable body fluids, the grape juice now over-

flowing and staining her kitchen floor.[12] Together they form a
river in her mind to which she gives the ancient name
'Meneseteung':

> The name of the poem is the name of the river. No, in fact
> it is the river, the Meneseteung, that is the poem – with its
> deep holes and rapids and blissful pools under the summer
> trees and its grinding blocks of ice thrown up at the end of
> winter and its desolating spring floods. (*FMY*, 70)

Almeda slips out of the safe spaces of home into the
wilderness space of her imagination, escaping from the orthodox
feminine role through writing – or rather, imagining writing – a
new kind of visionary poetry about the Canadian wilderness
which is beyond words: 'a flow of words somewhere, just about
ready to make themselves known to her. Poems, even' (*FMY*,
69). Munro is situating Almeda within the tradition of English–
Canadian women's wilderness writing.[13] However this vision
seems to spell the silencing of Almeda for we hear no more of
her till the *Vidette* record of her death from pneumonia caught,
ironically enough, after being chased by some louts into the
Pearl Street bog. (Again, as Margaret Atwood claimed in *Survival*
or 'Death by Landscape' the wilderness has claimed another of
its victims.) The newspaper refers to her as a *'familiar eccentric,
or even, sadly, a figure of fun'* (*FMY*, 71). Almeda has become
an outsider in her own town, though the obituary goes on to
restore to her the femininity and poetic reputation (*'with a
volume of sensitive eloquent verse'*) which she has plainly
abandoned. Whether Almeda ever 'found' herself, having
succumbed to the ambiguous spell of the wilderness we do not
know; all we witness in this reconstruction is her moment of
cutting loose from Victorian conventions. Rather like Aritha van
Herk's heroine in *No Fixed Address*, crossing over the frontier
into wilderness territory makes it impossible to send back any
messages at all.

The story ends with a return to the present as the narrator
records her researches in the graveyard where she manages to
find Almeda Roth's stone, marked with the one word 'Meda', in

its place beside her parents and brother and sister in the family plot, unearthing it by 'pulling grass and scrabbling in the dirt with my bare hands' (FMY, 73). Evidently the contemporary narrator shares the historian's impulse to rescue obscure details from the past and to make connections, though in the last paragraph she seems to wish to withdraw from responsibility for the story she has just told, admitting she has made up the details of Almeda's life by inference only:

> And they may get it wrong, after all. I may have got it wrong. I don't know if she ever took laudanum. Many ladies did. I don't know if she ever made grape jelly. (FMY, 70)

It is that final disclaimer (absent when the story was first published in *The New Yorker* in 1988 but added to this version)[14] which foregrounds Munro's own hidden agenda as a woman writer, for the image of the swollen cloth bag full of grape pulp, the plop of the juice into the bowl, and the immovable purple stain on the kitchen floor when the basin overflows, provide the real connection between the story fragments. This connection highlights not femininity and 'the proper lady' but femaleness, linking a woman writer's domestic tasks with her menstrual flow and the purple bruise on the drunken woman's naked haunch, so making visible the unspoken hidden connections which unite all women regardless of social class or historical time. We may even see such imagery as Munro's version of *écriture féminine*, a way of writing the biological rhythms of the female body and so moving through metaphor beyond the body into the spaces of imagination, for grapes (even when made into jelly) carry connotations of the Bacchantes and their orgiastic worship of Dionysus, an ancient European female wildness as untamed as anything to be found in the Canadian wilderness. This emphatically fictive element of the grape jelly is the attribution of the contemporary narrator, so that her revisionist project recovers a great deal more than the name and voice of a forgotten nineteenth-century poetess. It uncovers connections (or should we say 'makes the connection'?) between women's bodies and writing within the subjective spaces of wilderness, reappropriating Canada's most popular cultural myth as the elusive site of the female imagination.

On the other hand, there is no re-visioning of the past through fresh eyes in 'Oranges and Apples' although the story is about looking back over thirty years of a marriage, possibly because there are no new critical directions available from which to read that old text but only repetitions with variations. This is another of Munro's ongoing domestic narratives of life in small-town Ontario – this time in Walley, the Goderich of 'Meneseteung' a hundred years on. It is not the story of a broken marriage, though its one extraordinary crisis in the mid-1960s seems to reflect some of the upheavals of that time which another of Munro's narrators recalls so vividly in 'Oh, What Avails':

> Many parents got divorced, most of them shipwrecked by affairs, at about the same time. It seems that all sorts of marriages begun in the fifties without misgivings, or without misgivings that anybody could know about, blew up in the early seventies, with a lot of spectacular – and, it seems now, unnecessary, extravagant – complications. (*FMY*, 207)

It is as if, according to the narrator in 'Friend of My Youth', these tendencies had 'come in spores on the prevailing wind, looking for any likely place to land, any welcome' (*FMY*, 23).

The title of the story refers to a childish though very dangerous game about impossible choices where nobody wins:

> The really hard choices could be between two things you liked very much or two things you disliked very much or between things that were for some reason almost impossible to compare. (*FMY*, 123)

Like a game, situations are enacted which are unreal and in the end abandoned: 'I give up. I can't stand it. It's too stupid. I don't want to think about it any more!' (*FMY*, 123). Yet the game with its temporary liberation from the everyday, creates free space for the play of unspoken desires and fears, opening up the familiar with glimpses into unfamiliar psychic territories which cannot be accommodated in real life and have to be forgotten in order to go on living. This story always seems to exist in potential, threatening to become something other than it is, either a disastrous story of forbidden love and betrayal or the story of a woman's fatal disease, though these dangers are averted and the action stays within the conventions of a respectable marriage which has lasted over thirty years. In similarly desultory fashion, the narrative seems to develop casually via a series of metonymic associations where driving through the countryside with his wife Barbara on the way to the doctor's in town, a middle-aged man called Murray Zeigler remembers a Polish immigrant named Victor Sawicky who used to live on a horse farm there but who moved away years ago to Montreal. However, such apparent randomness is only camouflage for an anguished narrative full of secrets and a possible infidelity while the story itself, told entirely from Murray's point of view, is actually carefully structured around two parallel incidents which occur thirty years apart. Indeed, different as they seem, there are striking similarities between this story and 'Fits' in *The Progress of Love*.[15] They are both told from the point of view of a middle-aged married man who is shocked and bewildered by a singular discrepancy in his wife's behaviour, so that he is forced to contemplate dimensions of unknowability within their familiar relationship. However, prospects of general upheaval are diverted in a homecoming at the end and the central enigma connected with his wife remains unsolved.

In this story Murray is faced with a second crisis in his marriage, for he is driving Barbara to the doctor's for the results of a biopsy on a lump removed from her buttock, which may or may not be a sign of cancer. As the doctor has already told them, the lump may be 'a floater ... a sealed message' which could well remain a mystery: 'The future is unclear till we know' (*FMY*, 113). It is this second possibility of losing Barbara which stimulates Murray to remember the summer when he thought that she would leave him for Victor Sawicky. In the telling, it emerges that Murray is a rather hapless individual who has lost his faith and also lost the department store in Walley founded by his great-grandfather, though he seems cheerfully 'competent and unfrazzled' as the owner–manager of Zeigler's holiday resort outside Walley where he and Barbara have lived ever since the 1960s. To all appearances this is a comfortable uneventful life, yet what emerges from Murray's own account is his incessant desire for drama – that same desire which we so often see in Munro's female narrators for more exciting plots than their own lives contain – and his tendency to romanticise people who appear to be more exciting than himself. He directs this adolescent 'capacity for worship' first towards Barbara, the Irish 'looker' as his father described her when she started working in the shop, and then towards the handsome Victor who strode into the shop one day like 'a golden palomino,' though 'of the two he found Victor far the more splendid and disturbing' (*FMY*, 114). It is Murray's peculiar talent to contrive theatrical spectacles to display his most prized possessions – either by modernising his shop in 1965 with classy eye-level windows 'as if intended to display the Crown jewels' (*FMY*, 110), or by arranging a dinner party to show off his wife and his new friend to each other – though in every case these efforts are a failure. (The word used in the story is 'insanity'.)

Perhaps it is within that context of failed expectations of high drama that we need to read Murray's account of the first crisis in his marriage when he suspects that Barbara and Victor are having an affair. Certainly one odd, striking event occurs that summer which is fatal to Murray's peace of mind when he comes home unexpectedly and finds his wife (as he might expect to see her) sunbathing in the back yard beside the paddling pool where their small son is playing. Struck with admiration for her ample body, Murray is observing her when he notices a slight discrepancy:

> Some pause or deliberateness, a self-consciousness, about that slight swelling and settling of the flesh made it clear to him – a man who knew this woman's body – that the woman wasn't alone. In her thoughts, at least, she wasn't alone. (*FMY*, 126)

As Murray's gaze shifts he sees Victor who is now their lodger looking out of his window on the third floor and notices that 'there was something odd about his face, as if he had a gas mask on' (FMY, 126). What follows is the most extraordinary image in the story, for Murray goes up to get his binoculars to look at Victor, only to discover that Victor is already looking through binoculars at Barbara:

> Murray could see himself – a man with binoculars watching a man with binoculars watching a woman. A scene from a movie. A comedy. (FMY, 127)

I repeat the image of this triangular pattern – this double spying – just as Munro does in her story, not only to focus on the sexual politics of the male gaze and the illicit pleasures of looking which are here confounded by the duplicities introduced by such duplication but also to hint at the distortions of vision which this elaborate voyeurism are likely to produce. How is Murray, or how are we as voyeurs seeing through his eyes, to interpret what he sees? Is Barbara providing as he thinks 'the most exquisite cooperation' by making herself into a spectacle 'obscene and enthralling and unbearable'? And what does it signify, even if she is? Might it not be like her passion for cheap flashy clothes which Murray has always believed to be nothing but a masquerade of sexiness? In other words, is Barbara 'lying' – and to whom – while she is lying beside the pool?

In any event, shocked by this apparent evidence of duplicity between the two people he idolises in his life, Murray allows himself to be consumed with jealousy. He says nothing to either Barbara or to Victor although they all meet for drinks almost every evening, but instead he becomes obsessed with telling himself a secret story about their infidelity which proceeds by instalments (all told in the present tense, in fragments and in italics) within the ongoing narrative of daily life. That life has now become a torment to him, 'a spiteful imitation of itself' (FMY, 129) though filled with a 'terrible elation'. Through a kind of dementia, Murray's altered vision interprets everything Barbara and Victor do as treacherous, distorted by his tale of '*the destruction of love'*. Like Othello with his 'occupation gone', Murray finds another occupation by inventing, or trying to invent, a dangerous game for his two protagonists to act out in his psychodrama. But is he like Othello, or is he like Leontes in *The Winter's Tale*? In either case he is the victim of his own madness.

Despite his stratagems Murray's plot-making is defeated and his climactic scene is foiled, though whether through innocence or duplicity he can never be sure. In a desperate attempt at plot resolution, he sends Barbara over to Victor's apartment one evening in late summer with a blanket. 'This is like a play,' he thinks as he goes into the kitchen to drink gin and await her return with the news that she is going to leave him: *'It's happened to me'* (*FMY*, 132). However the climax he so ardently desires is withheld. Evidently it does not happen, for at this point the story shifts ahead nearly thirty years to another occasion when Murray is waiting for his wife's return – this time from the doctor's in Walley.

Ambiguities are not resolved and no explanations have been offered, though as Murray waits at the bottom of the Sunset Steps beside Lake Huron for Barbara to appear – as she will do, walking down centre stage at the end – he notices a curious boulder on the beach. This boulder attracts his attention because of its formation, 'with a line through it as if it had been split diagonally and the halves fitted together again not quite accurately – the pattern was jagged' (*FMY*, 134). Murray speculates for a while on the boulder as mute witness of geological upheavals in the region at the time of the Ice Age: 'look at the way it had been folded, as well as split – the layer on top hardened in waves like lapping cream' (*FMY*, 134). Then he sits on the boulder and watches the lake, meditating on its waves as a metaphor for the passage of time and the passing of life, 'a washing away, a vanishing' as he remembers his father's death. It is surely the boulder which should attract the reader's attention. For all its solidity, it bears the traces of ancient fracture and knitting together again so that it offers itself within the story as a metaphor for the emotional upheavals and complexities within the Zeiglers' long marriage, which is also flawed but enduring.

Only when Barbara appears on the steps looking as opaque and secretive as ever to her husband, does the narrative flash back to the finale of Murray's old infidelity plot. When Barbara had reappeared that evening, she refused point blank to tell him anything about her encounter with Victor: 'We are never going to talk about it … We never will. OK?' (*FMY*, 135). And Murray had to agree. Next morning Victor departed on a bus out of their lives. Now, by a strange symmetry echoed in her language, Barbara dismisses Murray's worries about the results of the biopsy:

> 'I'm O.K.,' she says then. 'It wasn't anything. It wasn't anything bad. There isn't anything to worry about.' (*FMY*, 135)

She may well be telling the truth though we cannot be sure – just as she may always have been faithful to Murray. We might also wonder why Murray allowed himself to become so obsessed with jealousy, and whether perhaps he needed this threat of robbery to endorse his sense of Barbara's value – rather like those mythical burglars whom Del Jordan and her mother used to fear in their house out on the Flats Road: 'Their knowledge, their covetousness, made each thing seem confirmed in its value and uniqueness' (*LGW*, 92). An alternative explanation might be that Murray has always yearned for moments of certainty to give his life a sense of direction, even if it had to be the certainty of disaster. This possibility is curiously endorsed by his thought when he sees Barbara coming down the steps: '*Don't disappoint me again.*' Though he cancels out that thought when he realises that he does not really want his life to be like a tragic drama, the word 'again' connects the two moments of crisis in his mind.

And what of Barbara herself, who, for all her solidity and physical presence as his wife and the mother of his children, remains a rather mysterious figure in Murray's narrative? Of course he is familiar with her habits, her body, her silences, but just as she sometimes slips away without explanation from him and their guests at the resort or immerses herself deeply in the

books she reads, so she steadfastly preserves her own secrets –
though to her they may seem truths so obvious that they do not
need to be elaborated upon.

So Murray and Barbara stand together at the bottom of the
steps, reading a message attached to a boy's balloon which has
floated in all the way across the lake from Crompton, Illinois –
not a 'sealed message' this time, though according to Barbara
one not be trusted anyway. The story ends with her character-
istically dismissive comment, 'That's a lie' (*FMY*, 136). This is a
curiously disturbing ending for a story whose major focus seems
to have been on the attempt to sift truth from deception, but
there is no way for Murray (or the reader) to ever know more
than he does now. Maybe he already knows all there is to know.
The only possibility for Murray is acceptance 'in the long-
married way' of what may be only a comforting illusion – about
his wife's health now or her faithfulness in the past. This is an
acceptance which he has come to see as necessary in the face of
those universal life processes of washing away and vanishing
which he has already acknowledged beside the lake. Like
Oranges and Apples, life is a game which nobody wins.

Finally, faced with the lies, secrets and silences in Munro's
stories, and as we wonder if there is any end to deception,
revision and alternative versions, we may be reminded of
Adrienne Rich's comment in 'Women and Honor: Some Notes
on Lying'. It would seem to provide at least a partial explanation
for Munro's storytelling method in this collection:

> In speaking of lies, we come inevitably to the subject of
> truth. There is nothing simple or easy about this idea.
> There is no 'the truth,' 'a truth' – truth is not one thing, or
> even a system. It is an increasing complexity ... This is
> why the effort to speak honestly is so important. Lies are
> usually attempts to make everything simpler – for the liar
> – than it really is, or ought to be.[16]

Taking risks: *Open Secrets*

It's pointless to go on if you don't take risks. While the stories in *Open Secrets* have elements of mystery and romance for example, themes which have always attracted readers, they do not satisfy in the same way as a traditional mystery or romance would. As I stated earlier, I wanted these stories to be open. I wanted to challenge what people want to know. Or expect to know. Or anticipate knowing. And as profoundly, what I think I know.[1]

THE stories in Munro's latest collection would seem to be full of surprises with their introduction of a ghost, a spaceship and visionary experiences, but really all that is happening is another of those 'shifts of emphasis that throw the storyline open to question' (*BM*, 177). The alternative realities glimpsed here offer the same challenge to the limits of realistic fiction as her stories have always done with their mapping of mysterious worlds on 'the other side of dailiness', though now it is more difficult to separate reality and fantasy because different dimensions of experience appear to overlap. These stories represent Munro's perception of life as 'many-layered. And in a way, nothing that happens really takes precedence over anything else that happens.'[2] This rejection of traditional priorities and readerly expectations is a new kind of risk-taking, for 'the stories in *Open Secrets* aren't about what they seem to be about. Clearly some people find this quite disconcerting.'[3]

The referential framework of real life in small-town Ontario is still in place, as are Munro's interests in local history and the seductiveness of gossip about love affairs and scandals and occasional startling deaths – all those open secrets which she insists on telling. Incidentally, the concept of the 'open secret' is emblematic of the ways of small-town life anywhere, where everybody notices everything but nobody talks about it except in whispers. (It would be difficult to have open secrets in a city where things are either secret or else they are public knowledge, for cities do not nourish what Jane Austen so aptly described as 'that neighbourhood of voluntary spies' (*Northanger Abbey* (1818)) to be found in a village.) Of the eight long stories here, I shall discuss the title story, set like so many others in this collection in the town of Carstairs, plus 'A Wilderness Station' which is about Canadian pioneer history, and one of Munro's rare Australian stories 'The Jack Randa Hotel'. Together they might be classified as a mystery, a murder, and a romance, though every one of them is apparently so digressive and disrupted with so many shifting narrative perspectives and time frames that such generic distinctions slide into insignificance.[4]

'Open Secrets' is about a local event which is made into a popular ballad that does not have a satisfactory ending. Reported in the newspaper and retailed as gossip, it is the story of the disappearance of a teenaged girl called Heather Bell during the annual weekend hike of the Canadian Girls in Training. (The C.G.I.T. is an organisation similar to the Girl Guides in the UK.) Did Heather Bell drown in the Peregrine River Falls, or was she murdered, or did she simply hitch a lift out on the highway and go away? We never know because no trace of her can ever be found. The challenge is how to tell that story. The way Munro does it is to plot points on a topographical map of Carstairs with its shady streets, its town hall and its post office, moving further out to farmhouses and open land, but then to focus on what is left out of this map. How are the townspeople or the readers to interpret the blank spaces on the map where clues are deliber-ately obliterated? All we are left with are isolated pieces of evidence which cannot be pieced together to make any case in a court of law and with only a woman's flash of intuition as she looks out of her window at two people sitting on a wall beside the Pioneer Park. The mystery remains unsolved; the missing girl's photograph posted in public places starts to fade and eventually the story is dropped from the paper because of the editor's opinion that it 'can't be rehashed forever'.

Though told from no single point of view (and apparently held together by snatches of the ballad of Heather Bell's disappearance) the major focalisation is through the perspective of a youngish middle-aged woman called Maureen, one of Munro's local girls who has made good by marrying her employer, this time Lawyer Stephens. Much of the action takes place inside the Stephens' house overlooking the town square, where the story is retailed first by Maureen's cleaning woman and then by the 'Corset Lady' Marian Hubbert who comes with her husband to consult with the lawyer after breakfast one morning about the odd behaviour of an eccentric old man called Mr Siddicup, hoping it might provide a clue to the Heather Bell mystery. It is through these reports and Maureen's interior narrative that the story takes shape. In the process of telling, the story of Heather Bell is interwoven with Maureen's memories as a young girl and then later as wife of the ageing and difficult old lawyer who has recently suffered a stroke. It is her flash of intuition which provides partial illumination of the mystery – and of other mysteries as well. The problem is to make the connections between such apparently different narrative strands. (We may remember the father's remark in 'The Moons of Jupiter': 'The answer's there, but I can't see all the connections my mind's making to get it,' *MJ*, 225.) Connections would seem to lie in unexpected parallels between different people's lives; some of these are perceived by the characters themselves while others are only revealed by the way the narrative is pieced together. When told of Heather Bell's boisterous behaviour at the Hubbert farm on the way to the hike, Maureen remembers how she was once like Heather Bell in her own girlish giddiness on identical C.G.I.T. hikes, though 'of course you didn't vanish' (*OS*, 140). However the most remarkable connection is the one that centres on Maureen's view from her upstairs window of their departing visitors as she watches Marian Hubbert's husband stroking his wife's brown feathered hat (as if it were 'a little scared hen') and the woman's hand clamped down over his like an exasperated mother's. It is that sight which shocks Maureen so that she feels 'a shrinking in her bones' (*OS*, 154) for all the world as if she has suddenly caught sight of the murderer of Heather Bell. The odd word here is 'abhorrence' which Maureen attributes to Marian, though it strikingly connects with what follows in the next section, which reveals Maureen's own complicity in the guilty secret of her sexual humiliations at her husband's hands. It would seem to be her own experience which sensitises her to possibilities of male violence and to what Munro in an interview described as the ways 'women adapt to protect men'.[5] All through her husband's assault Maureen is remembering the sight of that other husband and wife with the feathered hat, and more obscurely she is thinking about making a custard for lunch. (Hen's eggs and mother's milk would seem to be the associative links in her mind.)

Restored later to the peace of her kitchen, Maureen does proceed to make the custard though she does it in the peculiar context of visionary experience. This is a good example of Munro's risk-taking and widening of imaginative focus as she follows her speculative interest in mapping alternative realities, 'as if there might be a life going on parallel to our lives to which we have only occasional access. So the stories probably are much more mysterious, and perhaps more difficult if you're reading from a realistic point of view.'[6] Remembering those C.G.I.T. hikes and the leader's claim to have once seen Jesus, Maureen considers her own occasional moments of vision when she imagines she sees into an alternative life that she might have been leading herself ('just a fluke, a speedily corrected error'). Now she imagines that she sees not the man's hand stroking the feathers but a man's hand being 'punished' – 'pressed down on the open burner of the stove where she is stirring the custard in the double boiler' (*OS*, 159). Her vision of a guilt acknowledged is all that happens, and the story shifts at the end into a future frame beyond the present situation. Far away from Carstairs, as the narrator informs us, Maureen will still be making custards and watching the 'soft skin form on the back of a wooden spoon and her memory will twitch', but the explanation for her flash of insight (if that is what it was) will never become plain. Increasingly Munro's characters have what appear to be revelations but they remain untranslatable; things are seen, but they are not understood.

This story circulates as gossip in its search for meanings within the social maps of everyday life, and though it does not solve the mystery of Heather Bell's disappearance, it does uncover all kinds of grotesque behaviour hidden behind closed doors – socially unspeakable events and odd parallels between respectable citizens and obvious eccentrics in this small town. Somebody must have seen something but nobody can or will say what they have seen, and finally the story becomes stale news: 'Heather Bell will not be found. No body, no trace. She has blown away like ashes' (OS, 159). It is a failed plot like so many stories in real life, but the telling exposes so much that is usually kept to the margins of social intercourse that Maureen's sense of bafflement in the last sentence assumes the status of metafictional comment on the narrative enterprise itself. Not surprisingly, we find embedded here not only the title of this story but the title of this collection: 'She seems to be looking into an open secret, something not startling until you think of trying to tell it' (OS, 160).

Like 'Open Secrets', 'A Wilderness Station' also baffles the reader though for different reasons, because this time there are multiple circumstantial accounts of a death (was it a murder?) that took place in rural Ontario in the 1850s, so giving the lie to the Carstairs newspaper editor's opinion that 'a story can't be rehashed forever.' 'A Wilderness Station' belongs to the sub-genre of pioneer narratives like 'Heirs of the Living Body' (LGW), 'The Stone in the Field' (MJ), and more recently 'Meneseteung' (FMY), looking back into the history of settlement in Canada West in which Munro's own ancestors participated. She draws on her Scots–Canadian inheritance of family memories and her father's novel The McGregors: A Novel of an Ontario Pioneer Family (1979), though like Del Jordan in Lives of Girls and Women she prefers to chronicle – or to invent – the untold stories that lie hidden like dark secrets within the body of official history.[7] As in those other stories, Munro reconstructs the local history of a place through the imagined words and lives of characters from a past which as she says, 'you have to think twice about regretting' (*MJ*, 35).

Though many of the stories in *Open Secrets* contain transcripts of letters within their structure this is the only epistolary narrative, being composed of eleven letters written over a hundred-year period, plus one newspaper article of a pioneer's recollections. There is no editorial framing device, so that we have a sense of the physical presence of a past which comes to us unmediated. The letters date mainly from the 1850s though the pioneer's recollections were written for publication in 1907 and a supplementary perspective is provided by the final letter dated 1959. This documentary material has been assembled by an unknown person, possibly the recipient of the last letter, a 'Mr Leopold Henry' of Queen's University, Kingston, who is writing a biography of Treece Herron MP, whose grandfather George Herron is one of the story's major protagonists. Commenting on visual effects in the epistolary novel, Elizabeth Heckendorn Cook remarks, 'The indispensable fiction of the letter narrative is that behind the volume you are reading, almost visible through the bars of print on the page, are the original personal documents from which the printed page has been impersonally, typographically transcribed.'[8] Munro's story presents a fiction of social exchange where letters are sent, unsent, and returned. Beginning with the reply to a letter previously received (which we do not see), it interweaves letters of different kinds, from the semi-official correspondence between a Presbyterian minister and a Clerk of the Peace – similar to a Justice of the Peace in the UK – to private letters from the female protagonist to a woman friend, as well as public and semi-public reminiscences written fifty or a hundred years later. The impression we have is of hearing the authentic voices out of which colonial history has been made. What do they tell us about life in Canada a hundred years ago? This multi-voiced reconstruction employs all the conventional elements of pioneer narrative: clearing the bush and building a log hut, the privations and dangers in the life of a settler or a missionary and the survival of the fittest, together with accounts of those orphan immigrants male and female who moved into the Canadian wilderness in the mid-nineteenth century, either by choice like the Herron brothers Simon and George or who were coerced into it by marriage like Annie McKillop who became Simon's wife. Wilderness narratives tend to be of two opposite kinds: stories of death and disaster or stories of survival, frequently accompanied by new freedom and prosperity, suggesting the status of wilderness as Canadian cultural myth as I have argued elsewhere.[9] Indeed we have examples of both kinds of narrative here, for two men die in the wilderness (Simon Herron and the Revd Walter McBain of the Glasgow Mission) while George Herron lives to write his reminiscences fifty years later. However, it is a woman's narrative which offers an interesting variant on this traditional pattern. Annie Herron, Canadian born daughter of Scottish parents who is taken from the orphans' home in Toronto to the backwoods of the Huron Tract, not only seems to feel quite at home in the wilderness but ironically lives a long life of freedom and safety by choosing to go to gaol. Annie survives to have the last word in the story. Evidently the wilderness myth is open to multiple interpretations, but then so are historical events as this story also demonstrates.

The major event recorded in these letters is the death of Simon Herron, which we first hear about in his brother's reminiscences published in the Carstairs *Argus* in 1907. George recalls Simon's accidental death from a falling tree in 1852, the way he dragged the body home through a snow storm, the domestic burial by himself and his sister-in-law Annie, and a blessing over the grave later from the Revd McBain when the weather cleared. A letter from the minister written in 1852 endorses this story, though it is contradicted by Annie herself. According to the Clerk of the Peace in Walley, Annie Herron walked into the gaol some months later claiming that she had come to confess to the murder of her husband whom she had hit on the head with a rock. Nobody believes her and she is regarded

as either lying or insane but certainly not criminal. Indeed there
are various theories about Annie's condition advanced by Revd
McBain and the prison doctor as the voices of patriarchal
authority, spiritual and secular; McBain believes that she is mad
with remorse because she was an unsubmissive and unchristian
wife, while the doctor opines that her delusions are the result of
reading too many romantic novels. We might say that there is
method in her madness for Annie manages to achieve her aim,
which is to take up residence in Walley Gaol as a kind of
permanent lodger. As she writes to her friend Sadie Johnstone in
Toronto, she feels 'pretty well and safe' in the gaol: 'I am safe
from George here is the main thing' (*OS*, 215). This odd remark
is explained in a third letter to Sadie (uncensored apparently and
not sent through the prison authorities) where Annie offers yet
another version of Simon's death. She says he was murdered by
George who hit him on the head with an axe in a fit of anger at
Simon's ill treatment. Annie comforts and protects George, but
she adds in her letter that after the burial she suffered such
terrible nightmares about being attacked by him that she had to
flee into the wilderness 'and God protected me'. As winter
approached she decided to seek shelter in the gaol. Of course
Simon's body is long since buried and as Canadian critic George
Woodcock remarked: 'We end up never quite knowing who is
telling lies about the death of Simon Herron. Was it his brother
with an axe? Was it his wife with a rock? Was it a falling branch
hitting him on the head and killing him instantly?'.[10] Almost
certainly he was not killed by a bear, though that is another
suggestion made by Annie when she talks about her life in the
wilderness fifty years later.

The effect of such slippery narration is to shift the reader's
interest away from the event and to focus instead on the
storytellers, especially on Annie. She is an oddly itinerant figure
in the men's stories; introduced merely as a useful commodity
('a female suitable to his needs' as the Revd McBain describes
Simon's bride), Annie walks out of George's narrative after his
brother's death. She might be said to walk through McBain's
letters to the prison officer in Walley, a kind of wild woman with

eccentric habits of sleeping outdoors and refusing all Christian help and guidance. When Annie walks back into the narrative with her arrival at Walley gaol, we may well be surprised to find such an imaginative and God-fearing young woman whose own narrative hints that the real threats to her come not from nature but from men. Her 'madness' looks not so much like wayward-ness as a conscious policy of resistance to male authority and violence, where storytelling is her prime survival strategy. Annie becomes a kind of Scheherazade figure rather like Grace Marks in Margaret Atwood's novel *Alias Grace*, which is another nineteenth-century woman's prison narrative where truth is so scrambled with falsehood that it remains forever elusive. For these women, storytelling is not about revealing secrets but rather about keeping them while managing to stay alive.

Annie's life story has a happy ending as we learn from the letter written in 1959 by Miss Christena Mullen, the Walley prison officer's granddaughter. She recalls taking 'Old Annie' for a drive in her new steam car in 1907 to visit Annie's relatives, the now prosperous Herron family in Carstairs. Annie had continued to live in the gaol as a sewing woman and then later moved to the prison officer's family as a domestic servant, delighting everyone with her crazy tales: 'Don't get Old Annie going ... And don't believe a word she says' (*OS*, 218). That visit is Annie's moment of glory, a kind of comic apotheosis as she sits in the car dressed up like a queen in plum-coloured silk, speeding along silently on clouds of steam, for 'the Steamer covered the miles like an angel' (*PS*, 219). She enters the stately home of the Herrons like an honoured guest and sits for a couple of hours with George. By now he has become a patriarchal figure with a long white beard, though he has lost his voice as the result of a stroke and Annie is able to tell the story her own way without contradiction. We never know what she told George, though the sight of the two old people who have fallen asleep in each others' company suggests a moment of reconciliation at the end of a lifetime. The story ends with another of Annie's fanciful narratives about a baby who came to life like a ginger-bread man in an oven, which provides an appropriate context for her last comment of all where truth seems to be woven into the crazed patterns of fiction: 'I did used to have the terriblest dreams' (*OS*, 225).

'A Wilderness Station' is another way of writing history, using documentary evidence with no visible narrative reconstruction beyond the arrangement of the documents themselves. Yet nothing could more convincingly demonstrate the fictive nature of historical narrative than these multiple versions of a death that occurred over a hundred years ago. As Hayden White remarks, 'No given set of events attested by the historical record constitutes a story manifestly finished and complete. This is as true of the events that constitute the life of an individual as it is of an institution … We do not live stories, even if we give our lives meaning by retrospectively casting them in the form of stories.'[11] It is that last sentence which leads us into Munro's decentred narrative method with the storytelling of Annie, George and Revd McBain, all of whom offer conflicting versions of a single event which encode their different approaches to life in general and to the Canadian wilderness in particular. For George, with his ethic of progress, the wilderness exists to be cut down and cleared in the interests of material prosperity; for McBain the Calvinist preacher from the west of Scotland the wilderness spells geographical and spiritual exile ('This world is a wilderness,' (*OS*, 204), while Annie with her more liberal Christian beliefs in a God of compassion, journeys through the wilderness towards a promised land (represented here in its secularised version by the Herron family's estate). While the letters catch the tone of nineteenth-century sensibilities which are different from our own they also register differences between those sensibilities, offering the reader alternative maps of wilderness places as symbolic territory. Indeed for readers in the 1990s the fascination of this story out of Canada's colonial past lies less in the raw materials of historical fact than in the transformations of fact which are coded into subjective responses to the wilderness.

'The Jack Randa Hotel' shifts the scenario from Canada to Australia, though it features a Canadian protagonist called Gail who travels all the way from the small town of Walley in Ontario to Brisbane in Queensland in order to track down her former lover who has married an Australian drama teacher. Should this story be classified as a romance? Is it another version of an epistolary narrative? Is it really a female travel narrative? Munro's irony mocks the limits of genre, for like her travelling heroine she too takes risks, shifting positions as she moves between realism and fantasy in a story that ultimately exposes the constant deferrals implicit in any discourse of romantic desire. Like Luce Irigaray who declared, 'I am attempting ... to (re)discover a possible space for the feminine imaginary,'[12] Munro outlines a similar project in many of her stories.[13]

'The Jack Randa Hotel' does provide a version of a woman's travel narrative, giving the specific details of Gail's preparations to leave Canada, her flight to Australia and her arrival in Brisbane, yet oddly her travelling functions less as a journey from one country to another than as a border crossing between real life and the exotic spaces of fantasy. There is a certain mockery in a travel story which opens with an account of the heroine's plane being grounded in Honolulu, and finally when she arrives in Australia it is 'the wrong time of day'. Such unforeseen disruptions may upset the reader's expectations or perhaps refashion them, for Gail is not so much a tourist as a woman on a romantic quest. Australia for Gail is 'elsewhere', an elsewhere defined by Will's initiative in leaving her and going to Brisbane, so that there is a constant slippage here between real places and fantasy. Brisbane may look real with its ridged residential streets around Toowong leading up from the muddy brown Brisbane River, where 'houses cling to steep-sided gullies full of birds and trees' (OS, 180), but for Gail it is also a surreal landscape where birds with names like 'galahs' and trees called 'jacarandas' are foreign to her. Moreover, Gail herself seems to have disappeared behind a disguise and several name changes: 'Would anybody know Gail? With her dark glasses and her unlikely hair, she feels so altered as to be invisible. It's also the fact of being in a strange country which has transformed her' (OS, 170). Just as vivid topographical details are transformed into backdrop scenery for Gail's fantasy, so the action of the Brisbane plot seems to follow fairy tale configurations of coincidence and inevitability. She becomes a violator of private property, then an impersonator of a dead woman and a forger, first stealing a letter from Will's mailbox outside his house and going on to invent a bizarre correspondence with him. This is not under her own name of course, but under the assumed identity of 'Ms Catherine Thornaby' to whom Will had written. (It is his letter to that woman marked 'Return to Sender, Died Sept. 13' and stolen by Gail which provides the mainspring for the mystery part of the plot.)

Munro's narrative method commands our attention here as the story moves from travel narrative to exchange of letters between Gail and Will, so '(re)discovering a possible space for the feminine imaginary'. Gail succeeds in finding a place from which she can speak to Will through fantasising herself as the Other, while the Ms Thornaby pseudonym allows her to appropriate Will's own surname by subterfuge. It is fascinating to look at the contents of their correspondence for these are not, as we might have expected, love letters at all. On the contrary they are negotiations about power where it is Gail who assumes a position of superiority over Will, writing fluently for the first time in her life from within her bossy Ms Thornaby persona. If we ask why Gail embarks on her complex act of ventriloquism we may gain some interesting insights into the feminine imaginary. It is obvious that speaking through the voice of the Other she would be able to voice the subtext of her jealousy and rage at Will's desertion, just as she would gain a voyeuristic thrill in fantasising a strange intimacy with him, but more surprising is the pleasure she takes in her 'fine nasty style' of writing. Clearly the feminine imaginary is capable of conceptualising other pleasures than 'talking about love'[14] – the pleasure of revenge for instance, or the pleasure of gaining the upper hand in a sexual relationship: 'Was she a person who believed that somebody had to have the upper hand?' (*OS*, 167).

The correspondence fantasy cannot be sustained for it is continually disrupted by real-life events which are interpolated in the spaces between the letters. Munro's narrative reminds us of that referential framework which remains intractably in place despite the artifice of the invented correspondence, for like Del Jordan, Gail realises that writing does not actually transform anything: 'It is a shock, when you have dealt so cunningly, powerfully, with reality, to come back and find it still there' (*LGW*, 247). What does Gail do all day between writing letters to Will and awaiting his replies? Fantasist though she may be, hiding inside someone else's identity as she hides inside the second-hand floral print dresses she wears, she too has an address. She is living not far from Will's house in the flat formerly occupied by the late Ms Thornaby though living there under another assumed name, 'Mrs Massie, from Oklahoma'. Inevitably, daily life in Brisbane introduces other figures who shaft across the spaces of Gail's fantasy scenario – like the gay couple downstairs through whom she learns strange new Australian words like 'galah' and 'Jack Randa' and with whose lives (or rather the death of one of them) her own life becomes entangled. Everything contributes to destabilising Gail's fantasy, even Will's letter with the news of his mother's death ('Gail knew that Cleata would die, but somehow thought that everything would hold still, that nothing could really happen there while she, Gail, remained here,' *OS*, 182). However it is the death of the old man downstairs who has been deserted by his lover which constitutes the crucial moment of breakdown. Through a devastating irony Gail finds herself trapped inside a speeding ambulance with the dying man, who formerly had resented her very presence. At that moment she sees Will for the first time in Brisbane, and leaping up to call to him she finds that she cannot release herself from the man's hand: '"He's still holding on to me," says Gail. But she realizes as she says this that it isn't true … Now it is she who is hanging on to him. His fingers are still warm' (*OS*, 187).

Munro catches the moment of death which is also the pivotal point of reversal for Gail, who suddenly realises that she is hanging on to someone – and something – which is already dead. Faced with the collapse of her fantasy and with Will's imminent discovery of her secret, there is nothing for her to do but to cross back again to Canada and into real life. She needs to escape from Will's words shouted ('so she imagined – believed') through her door: '*Love – need – forgive. Love – need – forever*' (*OS*, 188). Gail has travelled through to the other side of the story of romantic love, so that its key words are as emptied of meaning as the sound of hammers in the street: 'Words most wished for can change. Something can happen to them, while you are waiting' (*OS*, 188). Standing in the airport having survived two deaths and the death of love into the bargain, Gail has already begun to distance herself from her Australian escapade 'as if her whole time there had been a dream' (*OS*, 189).

   Though the story does not quite end at this point, I propose to leave it there for the moment to consider what possible motive could have driven Gail to stalk Will and what this might reveal about the feminine imaginary. Perhaps the key is lodged in a sentence quite early in the story: 'The real scene was hidden from her, in Australia' (*OS*, 168). Seeing Will's address on a letter to his mother, Gail sets out in pursuit of an enigma which is represented for her by his handwriting. (This would account for the apparent inevitability with which her fantasy scenario develops, based on a duplicitous exchange of letters.) What is it that she 'wants to know? Or expects to know? Or anticipates knowing'? Gail's fantasy of desire is motivated by absence – not only the absence of Will but also her absence of knowledge about his life. Of course, when she gets to Brisbane the 'real scene' is still hidden from her as 'The house where Will and Sandy live is hidden by a board fence, painted a pale green. Gail's heart shrinks ... to see that fence, that green' (*OS*, 171). Gail must have missed other 'real scenes' closer to home as well, like Will and Sandy's falling in love and their decision to marry, just as 'real scenes' continue to happen outside her vision while she is in Australia. As Munro reminds us, 'We rarely live beyond the one reality we define or choose for ourselves. Yet things happen simultaneously in the universe.'[15] Gail does not see Cleata's death nor the break-up of the gay couple's relationship nor even the old man's death although she is right beside him in the ambulance, for at that very moment her attention is fixed on

Will who is still beyond her reach. This story is characterised by constant deferrals, though perhaps the most remarkable one is Gail's action at the end when she leaves Brisbane in order to avoid anything like a 'real scene' with Will: 'What she has surely wanted. What she is suddenly, as surely, driven to escape' (OS, 189). This signal of the fissure at the heart of romantic fantasy seems to me one of Munro's most significant insights into the territory of the feminine imaginary: 'It was a miracle, it was a mistake. It was what she had dreamed of; it was not what she wanted' (BM, 81).[16]

If this story seems to be structured around romantic fantasy and its collapse, there is also a possible 'Third Meaning', which is a kind of supplement coded into the narrative through its images.[17] I am referring to two distinctly Australian emblems here: the jacaranda trees and the box painted by the Aborigines, both of which provide a glimpse of another reality beyond the limits of the immediate action. When Gail sees the jacaranda trees in full flower outside the noisy Brisbane hotel she perceives it as a moment of grace:

> The flowers are a color that she has seen and could not have imagined on trees before – a shade of silvery blue, or silvery purple, so delicate and beautiful that you would think it would shock everything into quietness, into contemplation, but apparently it has not. (OS, 180)

Such miracles are on display, though they do not seem to make any difference to human behaviour apart from giving a name to the 'Jack Randa Hotel'. The other Australian emblem derives not from nature but from art, being the small Aboriginal-painted box which Gail buys in the airport shop:

> She picks out one that has a pattern of yellow dots, irregularly spaced on a dark-red ground. Against this is a swollen black figure – a turtle, maybe, with short splayed legs. Helpless on its back. (OS, 188–9)

Strategies of representation are complex in the final movement of this story. Gail's attention is focused on the yellow dots which remind her of the Huron butterflies she and Will once saw together, just as they represent her desire for an impossible moment of stasis outside time. Something Gail does not contemplate (possibly because it is too painful) is the black helplessly floundering creature also in the picture. Surely there is an element of self-mockery here, for Gail's own body has been represented throughout the story as grotesque. Not surprisingly, when she finally turns against Will she decides to send him the whole package: her romantic fantasy together with its unwriting, all graphically illustrated in a foreign idiom – to be accompanied by a challenge in her own hand: '*Now it's up to you to follow me*' (*OS*, 189).

So deliberating, Gail thinks forward to when she will send the Australian artefact back to Will from Canada, turning the whole romantic quest into a mocking game of hide-and-seek. One question remains: why does Gail want to continue this game beyond the collapse of her fantasy of desire? Has she learned nothing through her Brisbane experience? Thinking of the names of the Australian trees and birds which Gail does not quite catch, we may recall the words of Will's mother about *The Anglo-Saxon Chronicle* and the Dark Ages: 'We could not remember anything we did learn, and that was because of the names' like Cædwalla and Ælfflaed (*OS*, 164). Even after the collapse of romantic fantasy Gail has apparently not remembered enough to position herself otherwise in her discourse of desire. She does not move outside the closure of traditional romance plots but merely tries to reverse the roles in order to ensure that the story keeps going on. There is a kind of forlornness about this scenario of the feminine imaginary which would seem to confirm what Irigaray is in revolt against: 'So there is, for women, no possible law for their pleasure. No more than there is any possible discourse.'[18]

Munro's story is open to the risk of this interpretation, but let us not forget that 'Third Meaning' coded into those images from nature and art of something else beyond the contradictory discourses of realism and of fantasy: 'Form is never stationary or static. Much of the material might appear to be familiar but the security that familiarity offers the reader is illusory.'[19] If Munro takes risks to unsettle readers' expectations by showing us the limits of conventional plots of mystery and romance, she also takes the risk of showing unaccommodated moments of grace and insight which far exceed anything her characters or her readers might anticipate. There is a similar sense of 'radiant vanishing consolations' in 'Carried Away' and 'A Wilderness Station' as well as rare moments of blessing in 'Spaceships Have Landed'. These 'open secrets' signal new dimensions of the feminine imaginary which are made available to us through the spaces that open out within Munro's increasingly multilayered narratives.

Critical overview and conclusion

> Alice Munro is such a good writer that nobody bothers
> anymore to judge her goodness, as people long ago
> stopped judging [V.S.] Pritchett's – her reputation is like a
> good address.[1]

JAMES Wood's review of Alice Munro's *Selected Stories* is
praise indeed from the British literary establishment, but one
cannot help wondering how Munro herself would react to having
her fiction lifted into a position so securely beyond gender,
nationality and criticism. Her short stories have been widely
anthologised in Canada, Britain and the USA since the early
1980s in collections which variously highlight women's writing,
Canadian writing and postcolonial writing.[2] There have been at
least ten book-length studies of her fiction, and critical essays on
Munro have appeared not only in North America and Britain
but also in France, Germany, the Netherlands, Denmark, Spain,
Slovenia, Australia and India, all of which attests to Munro's
international reputation as one of the great short story writers
in English. However, although Munro had been publishing
stories since the 1950s and had won the Governor General's
Award in Canada in 1968, it was only after the popular success
of *Lives of Girls and Women* in 1971 that she became recognised
as a 'Canadian author'. The first signs of interest were several
groundbreaking interviews in the 1970s – John Metcalf's in
1972, Graeme Gibson's in 1973, followed in 1981 by J. R. (Tim)
Struthers's and by Geoff Hancock's in 1982.[3] These interviews
were concerned with introducing Munro to a Canadian readership

by giving autobiographical information, discussing literary influences and the distinctive qualities of her narrative art. They also elicited some interesting comments from Munro about her position as a short story writer in Canada in the early 1970s where writing short stories 'wins one so little respect'[4] and about being a woman writer with three small children: 'I've read about myself, you know, Alice Munro has produced little, and I think it's a miracle that I've produced anything.'[5]

The Munro critical industry did not take off till March 1982, when the first academic conference on her work took place at the University of Waterloo in her own region of south-western Ontario.[6] It resulted in a book of essays, *The Art of Alice Munro: Saying the Unsayable*, edited by Judith Miller (1984), though by then Louis MacKendrick's *Probable Fictions: Alice Munro's Narrative Acts* had already been published (1983). Together, these two books present an overview of Munro's major preoccupations in her first four books, mapping out the main directions for subsequent Munro criticism up to the present time. There have of course been shifts of emphasis in response to changing phases of literary and theoretical debate though the recurrent topics of critical interest have remained remarkably constant. The essays in Miller deal with the short story as a literary genre, the design of Munro's collections, and the way her language 'violates the familiar' by 'speaking about things not to be mentioned'. Several essays focus on her representation of women's experiences and a woman writer's relation to her literary inheritance, together with her use of paradox and narrative irony which 'hides the erotic in the respectable'. Harold Horwood's interview with Munro[7] focuses on her Canadianness, especially her concern with writing about rural Ontario: 'I love the landscape. It's just that it's so basic like my own flesh or something that I can't be separated from'. W. R. Martin's 'Hanging Pictures Together: *Something I've Been Meaning to Tell You*'[8] discusses the design of that collection and the intricate patterns of connection between stories; it was he who used the phrase 'barely felt gravitational pulls and ironic repulsions' to describe the tensions and cross-currents generated by Munro's story arrangements. James Carscallen's 'The Shining House: a Group of Stories'[9] is a somewhat idiosyncratic investigation of intertextuality which focuses on patterns of imagery, while essays by J. R. (Tim) Struthers[10] and Joseph Gold[11] foreground the metafictional dimensions present from her earliest work and her use of language as a means of imaginative entry into different worlds as well as an antidote to confusion. Already we see critical interest in Munro's storytelling attempts to capture and control reality through attention to surface details, while registering the significance of what Miller calls 'overlapping paradoxes' in her work. Barbara Godard's '"Heirs of the Living Body": Alice Munro and the Question of a Female Aesthetic'[12] is the first and still one of the best feminist essays on Munro. Beginning with the question 'How to write as a woman?' Godard addresses issues of female subjectivity and women's desire as well as a woman writer's relation to literary conventions, drawing most of her examples from *Lives of Girls and Women*. Focusing on Munro's strategies of 'proliferating alternatives' which serve to blur binary distinctions, Godard discusses intertextual encounters with a dominantly masculine literary tradition and Munro's parodic revisions of Milton, Keats, Tennyson and Joyce, in contrast to her use of the maternal tradition. Remembering 'the strength of lost mothers,' not only does Del Jordan the budding writer recall women's novels like *Wuthering Heights* or *Gone with the Wind* but she also works within the oral tradition of female gossip re-vising it to suit her own ends. As Godard shows, Munro's method for writing about girls' and women's experiences combines gossip with poetry, history and epic in Del's re-visioning of her dual inheritance: 'Writing from the senses, from the reality of her female body, she tries to bridge the gap between experience and a literary tradition which has objectified or effaced her sexuality. Mother's body, father's literature and language'.[13] This essay set the agenda for feminist criticism of Munro and I shall refer to it again, though there is one other important essay in Miller to be noted.

Useful information on research materials is provided in 'The Invisible Iceberg' by Jean F. Tener[14] which holds Munro's papers.

Calgary's Special Collections has had three Alice Munro Accessions since 1978 (now referred to as the Alice Munro fonds),
details of which are now available on the worldwide web.[15]

The major focus of *Probable Fictions* is on Munro's
narrative technique and style. Only one contributor's name
reappears from the Waterloo conference and that is J. R. (Tim)
Struthers, whose interview with Munro[16] provides an invaluable
source of information on Munro's writing methods and literary
experimentation over thirty years from the early 1950s, together
with some remarkable stories of the genesis of *LGW* and *BM*
(*Who Do You Think You Are?*). It was Struthers who first
explored Munro's affinity with women writers of the American
South and her fascination with the American Depression era
photodocumentaries of James Agee and Walker Evans, all of
whom like Del Jordan wished to 'record every last thing'. The
debate about Munro and realism is at the centre of this
collection, where Robert Thacker's much-quoted essay 'Clear
Jelly: Alice Munro's Narrative Dialectics'[17] and Catherine
Sheldrick Ross's '"At Least Part Legend": The Fiction of Alice
Munro'[18] analyse the ways in which documentary details split
open in these stories to reveal the 'powerful legendary shapes
behind ordinary life'. The same topics relating to double vision
and fictive artifice are explored from a feminist perspective by
Margaret Gail Osachoff in her discussion of the ambiguous mix
of autobiography and fiction in 'Treacheries of the Heart:
Memory, Confession and Meditation in the Stories of Alice
Munro'[19] and in Lorna Irvine's 'Changing Is the Word I Want'.[20]
Beginning with Del's mother's comments on body transplants
and her vision of change in women's lives, Irvine focuses on the
theme of transformation in Munro's fiction – the transformations in girls' bodies as they become adults and the possibilities
for transformation within social structures. She usefully points
to the importance of secrets within Munro's narratives,
indicating what would become a significant area of critical
inquiry: 'I suggest that the dominance of secrecy and alternate
texts in her stories implies an underground that is characteristic
of texts by women'.[21]

Irvine continued her investigation into Munro's re-visionings of traditional female romance narratives in a chapter 'Women's Desire/Women's Power: *The Moons of Jupiter*' in *Sub/Version* (1986), and several of these early critics have gone on to write major critical studies on Munro. W. R. Martin's *Alice Munro: Paradox and Parallel* (1987) examines Munro's fiction from her earliest uncollected stories up to those published by 1986. Martin offers close readings of individual stories and discussions of the published collections, with a focus on Munro's sense of irony and incongruity whereby oppositions are transcended in moments of vision. However, his tendency to want to find resolutions in Munro's fiction is sometimes defeated by the indeterminacy of the stories themselves.

Catherine Sheldrick Ross's 97-page book *Alice Munro: A Double Life* (1992) is the only illustrated biography of Munro to date, though there is a strong strain of criticism encouraged I would think by the numerous published interviews with Munro which emphasises the autobiographical dimension in all her fiction. The most subtle study of Munro's deliberately equivocal use of autobiographical material is Robert Thacker's '"So Shocking a Verdict in Real Life": Autobiography in Alice Munro's Stories' (1988)[22] which focuses usefully on her narratives as fictive attempts towards self-definition and on the relation between memory and imagination. Christopher Gittings's recent essay, 'Constructing a Scots–Canadian Ground: History and Cultural Translation in Alice Munro' (1997) initiates a promising new line of inquiry into Munro's fictionalising of autobiographical material with her 'transformative acts of memorialising family history' in her wilderness stories. Gittings's emphasis on the reconstruction of storytelling which 'destabilises the truth claims of the old master narratives of an ancestral past' points firmly towards the indeterminacy of Munro's fiction; it may be grounded in Canadian myths of origin but Munro reinvents those old stories to produce narratives whose meanings remain multiple and often contradictory.

Indeed it is Munro's elusive narrative art which has contin-ued to attract most critical attention, and two other books of the late 1980s tend like Martin's to focus on distinctive features of paradox in her work. In *The Other Side of Dailiness: Photography in the Works of Alice Munro, Timothy Findley, Michael Ondaatje and Margaret Laurence* (1988) Lorraine York discusses Munro's 'photographic vision' where scrupulously observed surfaces are dislocated by the narrator's powerful emotional responses. In her reading of Munro's fiction York pays close attention to the 'delicate moment of exposure' in both its photographic and its revelatory senses, drawing an analogy between the photographer's art and Munro's, as both attempt to fabricate order in the face of a recalcitrant reality which can only be partially grasped. Ildiko de Papp Carrington's *Controlling the Uncontrollable: The Fiction of Alice Munro* (1989) approaches the paradoxical enterprise from a different perspective when she argues for Munro's consciously ambivalent attempts to control what is uncontrollable in experience and in language. Focusing on recurrent metaphors of splitting and key words like 'shame', 'humiliation' and 'watch', Carrington presents a darker Munro, exploring her manipulation of point of view, techniques of retrospective narrative and voyeurism in her exposition of the paradoxical combination of power and powerlessness, secrecy and exposure experienced by female narrators both inside and outside fiction: 'To begin, she [Munro] defines the power of her artistic vision as the direct result of her lack of power as a woman'.[23] With its excellent chapters on 'The Humiliations of Language', 'Humiliated Characters, Voyeurs and Alter Egos' and 'Controlling Memory' this study manages to illuminate if not to explain the lingering sense of unresolved ambiguity and dismayed unease which is frequently the reader's response to these stories.

The 1980s fashion for paradox as the key to interpreting Munro's fiction seems to have been displaced in the 1990s by the concept of 'layering' which has been developed in very different ways by the Netherlands critic Charles Forceville and in Canada through the book-length studies by Ajay Heble and James Carscallen. Forceville's essay, 'Alice Munro's Layered Structures' (1993)[24] explores recurrent images of surfaces which always hide something else, tracing shifts from the local and the physical to the psychological layering of experience over time or the multiple versions of a story mediated by different narrators. Such a technique for analysing instability and unexpectedness would seem an appropriate critical response to the increasing complexities of Munro's late stories. Ajay Heble's *The Tumble of Reason: Alice Munro's Discourse of Absence* (1994),[25] which includes several stories to be collected in *Open Secrets*, is also concerned with the way that Munro's fiction with its constant deferrals and surprises subverts conventions of realism. Heble proposes a model of reading based on the multiple layers of meaning contained within language, where some meanings are explicit and others deferred or even indecipherable so that stories are always open to alternative interpretations. He develops the idea of a 'paradigmatic discourse' which he explains as 'Munro's awareness that for any utterance, for any claim to be inhabiting a particular realm of meaning, there are always potential levels of meaning, and alternative ways of formulating ideas and ordinary experiences, that must inevitably come into play.'[26] Though his exposition is rather cumbersome, Heble's concept of a 'fluid unresolvable alternation' of meanings is a persuasive critical tool which makes space for the parallel lives, significant absences and alternative versions which collapse distinctions between real and invented worlds in Munro's most recent work. To describe James Carscallen's approach in *The Other Country: Patterns in the Writing of Alice Munro* (1993) as another example of 'layered' criticism is perhaps not quite accurate for this monumental study adopts a method best described as 'imbrication', where overlapping layers of experience and complex patterns of allusion figure an elaborate system of correspondences. This is a fascinating and extremely difficult book, not least in its wide-ranging allusiveness and its inter-weaving of Munro's stories from all stages in her career, though there are very detailed cross-references and an index of stories and characters to orientate the reader. As Munro scholarship it will not easily be surpassed for Carscallen reads Munro's fiction as a kind of secular scripture, demonstrating his contention that 'her work offers us the great human myths, but as half-concealed – both from the characters themselves and from the reader – behind a surface ordinariness that seems anything but mythical'.[27] Any reader would profit immensely from the first section of this study where Carscallen explains his method of close reading for signs, literary allusions and associative patterns of imagery as stories shift between familiar and mysterious worlds. However, the main body of the book with its focus on the significance of names and its unearthing of Biblical parallels constitutes a very elaborate – perhaps over-elaborate – critical exegesis which is not for the undergraduate reader. My own critical reservation about this study is that is denies the randomness of life and that it shows no gender awareness at all, both of which seem to me distinctive features of Munro's fiction.

Turning now to the other significant strand in Munro criticism, feminist critics in the 1990s have developed many of the lines of inquiry which were opened up by Godard and Irvine. Beverly J. Rasporich's *Dance of the Sexes: Art and Gender in the Fiction of Alice Munro* (1990)[28] discusses Munro's fiction up to *The Progress of Love*, commenting on female romance fantasy, women's quests for independence and Munro's version of 'writing the body'. It is a carefully detailed reading, but the overall effect is one of paradigmatic feminist criticism which fails to get close the subtleties of these stories. Smaro Kamboureli's 'The Body as audience and performance in the writing of Alice Munro' (1987)[29] offers a much more theorised and exploratory reading of female body language in *Lives of Girls and Women* while Helen Hoy's 'Unforgettable, Indigestible Messages'(1991)[30] analyses with greater precision Munro's relentless scrutiny of female romantic fantasies within her representations of everyday reality, where 'reality proves more various than the human constructs created to contain it'. The major feminist study of Munro to date is Magdalene Redekop's *Mothers and Other Clowns: The Stories of Alice Munro* (1992). Redekop focuses her attention on Munro's obsession with mothers and mother–daughter relations, emphasising not paradox but repetitions and transformations of certain themes in a developing sequence throughout Munro's writing. Taking up Godard's question, 'How to write as a woman?' Redekop investigates the genre of women's fictive autobiography and the importance of the carnival-esque and comedy as new ways of thinking about auto-biographical form, where writing becomes a kind of circus performance or a series of clownings and self-parodies which make space for different ways of figuring female subjectivity. In detailed readings of five stories from every collection up to *Friend of My Youth* Redekop traces an emerging aesthetic which revolves around the composite figure of the mother (often a mock mother or an absent mother) and evolves through Munro's continuing experiments with narrative convention. Crucial to Redekop's feminist reading is Munro's comic vision where the woman artist is herself positioned within the circus parade of grotesques, always conscious of her trickster role: 'Like the conscious simulation of *trompe d'œil*, her stories clear an enchanted space within which, when you have finished reading,you can question the "reality" you live in'.[31]

Of the essays published in the 1990s on Munro's fiction, at least half have been devoted to the analysis of individual stories – convincing evidence of continuing critical fascination with Munro's narrative method. Robert Thacker's 1992 essay compar-ing Munro's story 'Dulse' with Willa Cather's 'Before Breakfast' reminds us of the complexity of any Munro story (not just her later ones) where no single line of analysis is anything but partial; not only are there likely to be many drafts of a story but also several published versions, while the multiple narrative strands render a story both lucid and resistant to interpretation. Faced with this challenge, it is not surprising that out of the thirty-nine essays on Munro since 1990 which I have read, twenty-one have been readings of single stories. Though several of these have been comparisons with stories by other Canadian or American writers, the passion for narrative analysis has taken precedence over the study of thematics, intertextuality and cultural or gender identity, though of course all these topics may be woven into close textual readings. (Exemplary models may be found in the essays by Ildiko de Papp Carrington, Helen Hoy,

Robert Thacker, Heliane Ventura and Kathleen Wall, listed in the bibliography.) Interestingly, several new essays signal a return to debates over Munro's realism, but critical ground has shifted so that the emphasis is on narrative artifice and the limits of realistic representation, like A. E. Christa Canitz and Roger Seamon's 'The Rhetoric of Fictional Realism in the Stories of Alice Munro' (1996).[32] Katherine J. Maberry's 1992 essay pays attention to Munro's anxieties about storytelling which highlight the 'uneasy discontinuous relation between narrative and experience ... the lies and uncertainties that no narrative can escape,'[33] while her 'Narrative Strategies of Liberation in Alice Munro' (1994)[34] speculates on the feminist implications of Munro's multi-voiced and multi-layered stories in ways that recall Godard's 1984 essay: 'Through her figuration of the narrative act as participatory, polylogic, and metaphoric, she frees the notions of truth and understanding from their association with control and dominance'.[35]

My main interest is in Munro's experiments with the short story form and her shifts of emphasis toward increasing indeterminacy and multiple meanings, always contained within a realistic and domestic framework. Two recent stories remind readers of her early comparison between a house and a short story, though with the difference that now there is less attention paid to the comforts of familiar surfaces and there is more speculation on the dark spaces inside and outside the house.

'What Do You Want to Know For?' is an autobiographical story where the telling of personal experience becomes a transformative act through which anxiety and mystery, though not explained away, are accommodated 'into the pattern of things we knew about' (p. 218).[36] Published in *Writing Away: The PEN Canada Travel Anthology*, this story is transformative in another way as well for it represents a reorientating of travel literature: Munro's journey is not to new and unfamiliar places but through home territory, 'the countryside that we think we know so well and that is always springing some surprise on us' (p. 208). Like so many of the characters in her fiction, Munro and her husband are driving along the highways and back roads in the countryside around Lake Huron, seeing not only the familiar roads but also what is off to the side and gesturing towards what cannot be seen at all. This is a story about buried secrets as the first sentence eerily indicates: 'I saw the crypt first, though it was in a cemetery to the left of the road, on my husband's side of the car' (p. 203). Even up close there is nothing to see except a stone arch and a grass-covered mound. The accompanying photograph shows the same surface details as Munro scrupulously describes them in her written account but gives 'no clues as to what might be inside', a phrase which might be taken as an emblem for this story. The idea of 'something strange', an 'unnatural lump' in the landscape which is associated with death, hovers over the narrative to chime uneasily with another 'unnatural lump' in the narrator's left breast which she reveals has shown up on a recent mammogram.

In this densely layered story parallels are suggested between landscape and the female body, an area of scholarship currently being explored by feminist geographers and literary critics.[37]   Munro however does not exploit the parallels for a feminist politics about possession or domination by the male gaze but instead she draws attention to the limits of gazing itself as an activity. What anyone sees is not all there is, for there are hidden secret places and buried stories within the most familiar bodily and geographical territories. Moving freely between bodyspace and landscape, she traces an alternative map of the countryside within the road map itself, referring to the 'special maps' which record the physical geography of southern Ontario with patches of vivid colour supplementing 'the usual roads and towns and rivers' and indicating the features of an ancient landscape formed during the last Ice Age. Only traces like 'eskers' and 'moraines' survive though they can be glimpsed if one looks closely enough, revealing a whole other world of 'little countries lying snug and unsuspected' (p. 208) beneath the seemingly unvaried agricultural landscape.

Munro is most excited however by those secrets which remain inscrutable to inquiry, and her story traces the stages of her double quest to find out the history of the mysterious crypt on the one hand and the nature of the lump in her breast on the other. Though this is more tightly structured than any other of her later stories, there are still gaps and digressions and surprising subsidiary revelations about buried or forgotten histories and places no longer marked on any map, not to mention the discovery of a second smaller crypt in the same cemetery as the first. The mystery of the crypt remains although the facts proliferate, for the narrator does her research in the university library and among the tombstones which she discovers to be those of late nineteenth-century German settlers in the region. However, although on a visit to the local Evangelical Lutheran church she is able to find out from the caretaker that the name of the German family who built the crypt in 1895 was Mannerow, the story at this point takes on the wonderfully digressive quality of gossip. In conversation, Munro discovers that the caretaker's husband had known her own father, and she explores the pleasure of that personal connection between present and past selves: 'He was happy to be reminded of himself as a young man ... I was happy to find someone who could see me still as part of my family' (p. 215). There is a further discovery inside the church which does shed a momentary radiance over the final part of the quest. On the walls are the texts in German and English of two Bible verses that had been painted over at the time of the First World War and were only revealed after a fire. The first verse is from Psalm 121:1 and the second from Psalm 119:105:

> I will lift up my eyes unto the hills, from whence cometh
>   my help.
> Thy word is a lamp unto my feet and a light unto my path.

The story at this point is full of promises of revelation, but is anything revealed or is there only another layer of mystery? As for the breast lump, the radiologist announces that it was actually there on earlier mammograms though nobody had noticed it, and she advises against any further investigation. 'You could be sure enough' that it was safe (p. 218). When they finally meet Mrs Mannerow she is happy to tell them as much as she knew about the crypt which she had seen the last time it was opened up. Inside the vault there was in addition to the family coffins a table with a Bible and a lamp on it, but now the crypt was full and would not be reopened: 'To think of it, sitting there just the same today, all sealed up and nobody going to see it ever again' (p. 220). Like the breast lump, this too remains a mystery. Did that lamp have any oil in it and would the space inside the crypt have been temporarily light or always dark? The biblical allusion widens the imaginative space but once again the answer is deferred indefinitely. Some secrets remain secret beyond the limits of sight, science or metaphysical speculation. So the story ends with a return to ordinariness (not unlike the ending of 'The Moons of Jupiter') as Munro and her husband drive home through the familiar landscape, with a sense of relief at the peacefulness of surfaces: 'Back where nothing seems to be happening, beyond the change of seasons' (p. 220).

By contrast with that ending, 'The Love of a Good Woman'[38] is obsessed with those 'deep caves' underneath the 'kitchen linoleum' (or in this case underneath the brown paint messily applied to the front-room floor), for this story bears all the hallmarks of Munro's scandalous Ontario Gothic tales: 'The dark stuff keeps coming back to me even now. You see, it hasn't gone.'[39] Subtitled 'A Murder, a mystery, a romance', the story does contain a mystery with the discovery of a man's body in the river near Walley; it also retails a dying woman's story about a murder, and it ends with a 'good woman's' desire for and expectations of romantic love – though all the genres are slightly off-centre here and like the stories in *Open Secrets* 'they do not satisfy in the same way as a traditional mystery or romance would.'[40] Framed by an anecdote about a box of optometrist's instruments in the Walley local history museum and the accompanying card about its owner, 'Mr D. M. Willens, who drowned in the Peregrine River, 1951', the story is focused through shifting perceptions, distorted vision and dark mirrors. The actual events of the narrative follow a tight chronological sequence, from the discovery of Mr Willens's body by three boys in early spring 1951 to the death of a young woman named

Mrs Quinn in July that same year. The story is not digressive although it gives that impression with its multiple narrative perspectives, its memory flashbacks and its sharp turning points, so that the mystery of the drowning is continually presented in new ways, each of which radically disrupts previous inter-pretations. In this clash of alternative versions distinctions between what is real and what is imagined tend to collapse and the dangers of hallucination are only dispelled, like the thick river mist, at the end.

There are many features here which might be investigated, like Munro's characteristic preoccupations with the intricate social geographies of small-town life and seasonal changes in the landscape, though my main concern is with trying to answer that question 'How to write as a woman?' by looking at one of her most recent explorations of female romantic fantasy. I believe this story sheds a fitful gleam on an earlier remark about the feminine imaginary in 'Bardon Bus': 'The images, the language, of pornography and romance are alike; monotonous and mechanically seductive, quickly leading to despair' (*MJ*, 123). The relation between two women – Enid the home nurse and her patient the dying Mrs Quinn – threatens to displace the opening mystery of the drowning, but the river runs through the story carrying the memory of the drowned man's body along with it as dark undercurrent in their fantasy lives. These female protagonists would seem to be opposites. Whereas Enid is a 'good woman' (a Christian who is devoted to her nursing profession: 'Her hope was to be good, and do good, and not necessarily in the orderly, customary, wifely way,' (p. 122)), Mrs Quinn with her sickly malfunctioning body is the person-ification of disorder, resentful, suspicious and 'deliberately vile'. At least that is how she is perceived by Enid, who is herself amazed at her own lack of compassion over this particular case. Mrs Quinn is one of those patients who refuse to 'settle down to their dying' with a good grace (in her twenty years' experience Enid has seen many) and a woman most likely to suffer from a diseased imagination. Yet the mystery remains: why does Enid dislike her so much, and why is there such a strong sense of mutual hostility between the two women?

Indeed it is Enid and not Mrs Quinn who suffers from nightmares when sleeping in the sick woman's room. As if the air she breathes is contaminated, Enid's dreams are filled with images of lust (copulations with 'utterly forbidden and unthinkable partners,' (p. 127)) so unnatural that Enid is tempted to think her sleep is invaded by the Devil, though that is a model of mind which she is inclined to reject as 'nothing but the mind's garbage', the dark unspeakable side of the feminine imaginary. Yet how can the contradictory impulses which seize Enid be explained? On the one hand Mrs Quinn's illness threatens to overshadow Enid's determined optimism and makes her efforts to do good look foolish while against that despair sounds a different message, this time from the General Confessional in the Anglican Book of Common Prayer:

> *Miserable offenders*, came into her head. *Miserable offenders.*
> *Restore them that are penitent.*[41]

Where does Enid's expression of her need for mercy and forgiveness come from? Is it her own mind which saves her or is it a message from elsewhere? As always in Munro such moments of grace remain ambiguous, and Mrs Quinn's daughter's childish question 'What does it mean "God bless"?'(p. 128) goes unanswered.

Mrs Quinn on the other hand refuses either priests or ministers just as she refuses the comfort of seeing her husband and her two young children. Instead in her last upsurge of energy before death she drags Enid into complicity, with her horrible tale about the murder of Mr Willens by her husband Rupert in the very room where she is lying. It is a scandalous tale of sexual transgression and male violence, elaborated to the last detail with her husband's disposal of Mr Willens's body by driving it in the dead man's car to the river bank then pushing it in: 'They said he was alive when he went in the water. What a laugh' (p. 132). Actually, Mrs Quinn's scenario is very close to Tay Garnett's film *The Postman Always Rings Twice*, starring Lana Turner

(1946) which she might well have seen as the events in the story take place in the early 1950s, but Enid does not think of that. Instead, under the powerful influence of Mrs Quinn's story she develops her own corresponding fantasy of forcing Rupert into a confession of murder by taking him out in a boat on the river and then visiting him when he is in prison. Indeed it is her fantasy of strange devotion to the guilty man which provides a crucial piece of evidence, not to the 'murder' but to the 'mystery' of her dislike of Mrs Quinn, her strangely celebratory feeling on the day of Mrs Quinn's death and also to the 'romance' of the subtitle.

Like everything else in this story, present time is only the surface of a many-layered past, just as places bear traces of their earlier history and families accumulate forgotten rubbish in cupboards or attics. Enid and Rupert are old schoolfellows, and interspersed with the story of Mrs Quinn's dying are the intervals when they re-establish their high-school friendship, itself built on a further layer of Enid's memory of her merciless teasing of Rupert and her own need for his forgiveness. For a 'good woman' like Enid any feeling of sexual desire for another woman's husband would be unthinkable, but those transgressive impulses are all attributed to Mrs Quinn. That 'casualty of the female life' with her diseased imagination becomes Enid's dark mirror as 'her horrible outpouring of talk' speaks all the things which Enid does not permit herself to think about while trying to 'be good'.

It is only after Mrs Quinn's death when Enid returns to take Rupert out on the fated boat trip that light breaks into her consciousness, just as it floods into the dead woman's empty room. As if an obstacle has been removed, Enid suddenly remembers something Mrs Quinn had said, '*Lies. I bet it's all lies*' (p. 138). That abrupt turning signals Enid's own radical shift of vision, as now she can envisage an entirely different future for herself and Rupert – not prison but marriage: 'What benefits could bloom. For others, and for herself' (p. 139). Mrs Quinn's tale of murder is not only discredited by Enid as 'a sick woman's fantasy' but it is steadily erased as she and Rupert walk together to the river. The mist has disappeared in the 'level dusty light of afternoon' as Rupert chops a path through the undergrowth down to the river where they find a rowing boat seen earlier by Enid 'riding in the shadows'. The story opens out into the space for a love story as Enid waits for him to find the oars: 'She could feel as if everything for a long way around had gone quiet.' The imagery suggests a journey to the promised land, where even the swarms of tiny bugs take on the shapes of clouds and pillars, reminding readers of the shape of the Lord's guiding spirit over the Israelites in Exodus.

Is this Munro at her most realistic or her most symbolic? The answer in this late story is as always double, for though this is realism it is also full of 'troubling distorted reflections' as reality is refracted through the narrator's subjective perceptions and desires, revealing not the total picture but only 'a patch of shiny silver' where a human hand has rubbed at the surface.[42] For all their increasing complexity and elusiveness, Munro's stories seem to me to follow an ongoing line of inquiry which was signalled in 'Walker Brothers Cowboy', the first story of *Dance of the Happy Shades* (which is also the first story in her *Selected Stories*). She has continued to investigate parallels between the instability of language and the incompleteness of any fictional structure on the one hand, and the indeterminacy of human relations and the excesses of the fiction-making imagination on the other. Her southwestern Ontario landscapes seem ordinary and familiar as we look at them, but her narrative art transforms them under our very eyes 'into something you will never know, with all kinds of weathers, and distances you cannot imagine' (*DHS*, 18).

News of the forthcoming publication of *The Love a Good Woman* arrived in the final proof stages of this study. With Munro, there is always a supplement.

Notes

Chapter 1

1 Alice Munro, 'Walker Brothers Cowboy', *Dance of the Happy Shades* (Harmondsworth: Penguin, 1983), p. 18.

2 H. Horwood, 'Interview with Alice Munro', in J. Miller (ed.), *The Art of Alice Munro: Saying the Unsayable* (Ontario: University of Waterloo, 1984), pp. 123–35.

3 J. Metcalf, 'Conversation with Alice Munro', *Journal of Canadian Fiction*, 1:4 (1972), 54–62.

4 Alice Munro, 'What Is Real?', in J. Metcalf (ed.), *Making It New: Contemporary Canadian Stories* (Toronto: Methuen, 1982); repr. in J. Metcalf and J. R. (Tim) Struthers (eds), *How Stories Mean* (Erin, Ontario: Porcupine's Quill, 1993), pp. 331–4.

5 'Alice Munro Interview', in G. Hancock, *Canadian Writers at Work* (Toronto: Oxford University Press, 1987), pp. 187–224.

6 Alice Munro, *Lives of Girls and Women* (Harmondsworth: Penguin, 1982), p. 249.

7 See Aritha van Herk, 'Mapping as Metaphor: The Cartographer's Revision', in *A Frozen Tongue* (Sydney: Dangaroo, 1992), pp. 54–68.

8 Alice Munro, *The Beggar Maid: Stories of Flo and Rose* (Harmondsworth: Penguin, 1980), p. 19.

9 See 'Baptizing', in *Lives*, 'The Beggar Maid', in *The Beggar Maid*, 'Bardon Bus', in *The Moons of Jupiter*, 'Meneseteung', in *Friend of My Youth*, and 'The Jack Randa Hotel', in *Open Secrets*, all of which I shall discuss in subsequent chapters.

10 Feminist criticism has focused on Munro's female aesthetic; classic pieces by Barbara Godard, Beverley Rasporich and Magdalene Redekop will be discussed in the critical overview at the end.

11 See Luce Irigaray, *This Sex Which Is Not One*, trans. Catherine Porter (Ithaca: Cornell, 1985) and also her essays on mother–daughter relations in M. Whitford (ed.), *The Irigaray Reader* (Oxford: Blackwell, 1995); and Rosi Braidotti, *Nomadic Subjects* (New York: Columbia University Press, 1994), to which I shall refer in my discussions of individual stories.

12 Classics of this criticism are Janice Radway, *Reading the Romance: Women, Patriarchy and Popular Culture* (Chapel Hill and London: University of North Carolina Press, 1984); Ann Barr Snitow, 'Mass Market Romance: Pornography for Women Is Different', in A. Snitow, C. Stansell and S. Thompson (eds), *Desire: The Politics of Sexuality* (London: Virago, 1984), pp. 258–75; Molly Hite, *The Other Side of the Story: Structures and Strategies of Contemporary Feminist Narrative* (Ithaca and London: Cornell University Press, 1989).

13 Cy-Thea Sand, 'Interview with Alice Munro', *Kinesis* (December–January 1983), 20–1.

14 Alice Munro, 'Bardon Bus', *The Moons of Jupiter* (Harmondsworth: Penguin, 1984), p. 123.

15 Margaret Atwood, quoted by Angela Miles, 'Confessions of a Harlequin Reader', in A. and M. Kroker (eds), *The Hysterical Male: New Feminist Theory* (Montreal: New World Perspectives, 1991), pp. 93–131.

16 Alice Munro, *Open Secrets* (London: Vintage, 1995), p. 50.

17 Jeri Kroll, 'Interview with Alice Munro', *LINQ (Literature in North Queensland)*, 8:1 (1980), 47–55.

18 Hancock interview, p. 191.

19 Alice Munro, 'White Dump', *The Progress of Love* (London: Flamingo, 1988), p. 308.

20 Catherine Sheldrick Ross, 'Interview with Alice Munro', *Canadian Children's Literature*, 53 (1989), 14–24.

21 Eleanor Wachtel, 'Interview with Alice Munro', *Brick*, 40 (Winter 1991), 48–53.

22 E. R. Epperley, *The Fragrance of Sweet-Grass: L. M. Montgomery's Heroines and the Pursuit of Romance* (Toronto: University of Toronto Press, 1992), p. 148.

23 Alice Munro, Afterword to *Emily of New Moon*, New Canadian Library (Toronto: McClelland and Stewart, 1989), p. 360.

24 Ross interview, p. 18.

25 Ross interview, p. 18.

26   Ross interview, p. 20.

27   Graeme Gibson, 'Alice Munro', *Eleven Canadian Novelists* (Toronto: Anansi, 1973), pp. 237–64.

28   Robert Thacker, 'Alice Munro's Willa Cather', *Canadian Literature*, 134 (Fall 1992), 42–57.

29   Alice Munro, 'Author's Commentary on "An Ounce of Cure" and "Boys and Girls"', repr. Metcalf and Struthers, pp. 185–7; quoted by Catherine Sheldrick Ross, *Alice Munro: A Double Life* (Toronto: ECW Press,1992), p. 45.

30   Stephen Smith, 'Interview with Alice Munro', *Quill & Quire* (August 1994), 1.

31   Alice Munro, 'Simon's Luck', *The Beggar Maid*, p. 177.

32   Alice Munro, 'Labor Day Dinner', *The Moons of Jupiter*, p. 144.

33   Smith interview, p. 24.

34   Dennis Duffy, 'Something She's Been Meaning to Tell Us', *Books in Canada*, 25:9 (December 1996), 8–10.

35   Only *Lives of Girls and Women* was ever published as a 'novel' and its omission from her *Selected Stories* would indicate that she wishes it to be considered as a novel.

36   J. Derrida, 'Structure, Sign and Play in the Discourse of the Human Sciences', in D. Lodge (ed.), *Modern Criticism and Theory: A Reader* (London: Longman, 1988), pp. 108–23.

37   Rosalie Osmond, 'Arrangements, Disarrangements and Earnest Deceptions', in C. A. Howells and L. Hunter (eds), *Narrative Strategies in Canadian Literature* (Milton Keynes: Open University Press, 1991), pp. 82–92.

38   Alice Munro, 'Open Secrets', *Open Secrets*, p. 162.

39   Wachtel interview, p. 52.

40   Wachtel interview, p. 52.

Chapter 2

1   'Alice Munro', in Graeme Gibson, *Eleven Canadian Novelists* (Toronto: Anansi, 1973), p. 248.

2   J. R. (Tim) Struthers, 'The Real Material: An Interview with Alice Munro', in Louis J. MacKendrick (ed.), *Probable Fictions: Alice Munro's Narrative Acts* (Toronto: ECW Press, 1983), p. 21.

3   'Alice Munro interview', in G. Hancock, *Canadian Writers at Work* (Toronto: Oxford University Press, 1987), p. 190.

4   Alice Munro, 'Winter Wind', *SIB* (Harmondsworth: Penguin, 1985), p. 193.

5   Only two stories in these collections have male narrators: 'Thanks for the Ride' and 'Walking on Water'.

6   Alice Munro, 'Images', *Dance of the Happy Shades* (Harmondsworth: Penguin, 1983), p. 43.

7   'Walker Brothers Cowboy', 'Images', 'Boys and Girls', 'The Peace of Utrecht' and 'Dance of the Happy Shades' appear in *Dance of the Happy Shades*; 'Something I've Been Meaning to Tell You', 'Material' and 'The Ottawa Valley' appear in *Something I've Been Meaning to Tell You*. All page references will be to the Penguin editions and included in the text.

8   Goderich is the real-life model for Tuppertown, though it is Wingham Munro's home town which has long been associated with country-and-western music; its local radio station CKNX was the first in Canada to broadcast these programmes.

9   Rosi Braidotti, *Nomadic Subjects: Embodiment and Sexual Difference in Contemporary Feminist Theory* (New York: Columbia University Press, 1994).

10 J. R. (Tim) Struthers, 'Alice Munro and the American South', in John Moss, *The Canadian Novel Here and Now: A Critical Anthology* (Toronto: NCL, 1978), pp. 121–33.

11 The Peace of Utrecht (1713) was significant for Canadian history for by that treaty France ceded to Britain its North American territories which in the words of the *Ontario Public School History of England* (1928) 'was the beginning of the British Canada of today'.

12 See Eve Kosofsky Sedgwick, *The Coherence of Gothic Conventions* (New York and London: Methuen, 1986), pp. 4–5; Robert Miles, *Gothic Writing 1750–1820: A Genealogy* (New York and London: Routledge, 1993), pp. 27–8.

13 Luce Irigaray, 'The Bodily Encounter with the Mother', in Margaret Whitford (ed.), *The Irigaray Reader* (Oxford: Blackwell, 1995), pp. 35–46.

14 Irigaray, 'The Power of Discourse and the Subordination of the Feminine', *The Irigaray Reader*, pp. 11–32.

15 Magdalene Redekop, *Mothers and Other Clowns: The Stories of Alice Munro* (London and New York: Routledge, 1992), pp. 50–57.

16 Redekop, *Mothers* offers the best and most sustained treatment of the mother–daughter topic in Munro's fiction, while Catherine Sheldrick Ross, *Alice Munro: A Double Life* (Toronto: ECW Press, 1990), pp. 38–41 sketches its autobiographical basis in Munro's mother's suffering and death from Parkinson's Disease.

17 Rosi Braidotti, 'Envy; or, With My Brains and Your Looks', in A. Jardine and Paul Smith (eds), *Men in Feminism* (London and New York: Methuen, 1987), pp. 233–41.

18 Alice Munro, 'What is Real?', in J. Metcalf and J. R. (Tim) Struthers (eds), *How Stories Mean* (Erin, Ontario: Porcupine's Quill, 1993) pp. 331–4.

19 Irigaray, 'Bodily Encounter', p. 34.

20 Irigaray, 'Women – Mothers and the Silent Substratum of the Social Order', *The Irigaray Reader*, pp. 47–52.

21 Irigaray, 'Bodily Encounter', p. 36.

22 The stories I shall treat which deal explicitly with the daughter's relation to the sick mother are 'The Peace of Utrecht', 'The Ottawa Valley' and 'Friend of My Youth.'

23 See Redekop's fuller analysis in *Mothers and Other Clowns*, pp. 103–14.

24 Irigaray, 'Bodily Encounter', p. 36.

25 Munro's quest to find an adequate representation of her mother bears striking similarities to Roland Barthes's efforts to represent his mother in *Camera Lucida: Reflections on Photography*, trans. Richard Howard (London: Vintage, 1993). I shall return to Barthes's text in my discussion of 'Epilogue: The Photographer' in *LGW*.

26 For a discussion of Munro's references to Tennyson's poetry, including his Arthurian romances, see Lorraine York, 'The Rival Bards: Munro's *Lives of Girls and Women* and Victorian Poetry', *Canadian Literature*, 112 (Spring 1987), 211–16.

27 Alice Munro, 'Author's Commentary on "An Ounce of Cure" and "Boys and Girls"', in Metcalf and Struthers (eds), *How Stories Mean*, p. 190.

28 Eudora Welty, 'June Recital' in *The Collected Stories of Eudora Welty* (New York and London: Harcourt Brace, 1982), pp. 275–330. For Munro's comments on her debt to *The Golden Apples*, see J. Metcalf, 'A Conversation with Alice Munro', *Journal of Canadian Fiction*, 1:4 (1972), 57.

29 Irigaray, 'Bodily Encounter', p. 36.

Chapter 3

1 Alice Munro, 'The Flats Road', *Lives of Girls and Women* (Harmondsworth: Penguin, 1982), p. 27.

2 Alice Munro, 'What Is Real?', in J. Metcalf and J. R. (Tim) Struthers (ed.), *How Stories Mean* (Erin, Ontario: Porcupine's Quill, 1993), pp. 331–4.

3 See C. A. Howells, *Private and Fictional Words: Canadian Women Novelists of the 1970s and 1980s* (London and New York: Methuen, 1987), for a longer discussion of realism and fantasy in *LGW* and *BM*, pp. 71–88.

4 Barbara Godard, 'Heirs of the Living Body: Alice Munro and the Question of a Female Aesthetic', in J. Miller (ed.), *The Art of Alice Munro: Saying the Unsayable* (Waterloo, Ontario: University of Waterloo Press, 1984), pp. 43–72.

5 J. R. (Tim) Struthers, 'The Real Material: An Interview with Alice Munro', in Louis K. MacKendrick (ed.), *Probable Fictions: Alice Munro's Narrative Acts* (Toronto: ECW Press, 1983), pp. 5–36. In her *Selected Stories* (1996) no material from *LGW* is included; evidently Munro would prefer it to be treated as a novel.

6 A. J. Gurr, 'Short Fiction and Whole Books', in C. A. Howells and L. Hunter (eds), *Narrative Strategies in Canadian Literature* (Milton Keynes: Open University Press, 1992), pp. 11–18.

7 Struthers, 'The Real Material', pp. 24–5.

8 'Alice Munro Interview', in G. Hancock, *Canadian Writers at Work* (Toronto: Oxford University Press, 1987), p. 201.

9 W. R. Martin, *Alice Munro: Paradox and Parallel* (Edmonton: University of Alberta Press, 1987), p. 21.

10 Hancock interview, p. 201.

11 My reading owes much to J. B. Harley, 'Deconstructing the Map', in T. J. Barnes and James S. Duncan (eds), *Writing Worlds: Discourse, Text and Metaphor in the Representation of Landscape* (London and New York: Methuen, 1992), pp. 231–47.

12 Struthers, 'The Real Material', p. 25.

13 Roland Barthes, 'The *Blue Guide*', in *Mythologies* (London: Paladin, 1972), pp. 81–4. See also J. S. and N. G. Duncan, 'Ideology and Bliss: Roland Barthes and the Secret Histories of Landscape', in *Writing Worlds*, pp. 18–37.

14 Aritha van Herk, 'Mapping as Metaphor: The Cartographer's Revision', in *A Frozen Tongue* (Sydney: Dangaroo, 1992), p. 63.

15   Godard, 'Heirs', p. 49.

16   Howells, *Private and Fictional Words*, pp. 81–4.

17   Rosemary Jackson, *Fantasy: The Literature of Subversion* (London and New York: Methuen, 1981), p. 65. For a psychological reading of the fantastic and discussion of Freud's essay 'The Uncanny' see pp. 61–91.

18   Struthers, 'The Real Material', p. 25.

19   Roland Barthes, *Camera Lucida: Reflections on Photography*, trans. Richard Howard (London: Vintage, 1993), p. 28. For a different treatment of photography in Munro see Lorraine York, *The Other Side of Dailiness: Photographs in the Works of Alice Munro, Timothy Findley, Michael Ondaatje, Margaret Laurence* (Toronto: ECW Press, 1988), pp. 21–50.

20   Barthes, *Camera Lucida*, p. 92.

21   Barthes, *ibid.*, p. 103.

22   Barthes, *ibid.*, p. 59.

Chapter 4

1   Alice Munro, 'Royal Beatings', in *The Beggar Maid: Stories of Flo and Rose* (Harmondsworth: Penguin, 1980), p. 10.

2   'Alice Munro Interview', in G. Hancock, *Canadian Writers at Work* (Toronto: Oxford University Press, 1987), p. 205.

3   Eleanor Wachtel, 'An Interview with Alice Munro', *Brick*, 40 (Winter 1991), 48–53.

4   Hancock interview, p. 203.

5   J. R. (Tim) Struthers, 'The Real Material: An Interview with Alice Munro', in Louis MacKendrick (ed.), *Probable Fictions: Alice Munro's Narrative Acts* (Toronto: ECW Press, 1983), p. 30.

6   See Helen Hoy, 'Rose and Janet: Alice Munro's Metafiction', *Canadian Literature*, 121 (Summer 1989), 59–83.

7   Much recent feminist theory is concerned with performance and identity as 'staged', e.g. Luce Irigaray's famous statement on female mimicry in 'The Power of Discourse and the Subordination of the Feminine', in Margaret Whitford (ed.), *The Irigaray Reader* (Oxford: Blackwells, 1995), pp. 124–5.

8   James Carscallen, 'The Shining Houses', in J. Miller (ed.), *The Art*

of Alice Munro: Saying the Unsayable (Ontario: University of Waterloo, 1984), p. 91.

9   Hancock interview, p. 204.

10 Luce Irigaray, 'Women's Discourse and Men's Discourse', in *Je, tu, nous: Toward a Culture of Difference* (New York and London: Routledge, 1993), p. 35. This essay has been a significant influence on my reading of fantasy discourses here.

11 Two other stories in this collection treat these affairs: with Tom Shepherd in 'Providence' and with Clifford in 'Mischief'.

12 Chris Weedon, *Feminist Practice and Poststructuralist Theory* (Oxford: Blackwell, 1987), 102.

13 Alice Munro, 'The Colonel's Hash Resettled', in J. Metcalf (ed.), *The Narrative Voice* (Toronto: McGraw-Hill Ryerson, 1972). Reprinted in J. Metcalf and J. R. (Tim) Struthers (eds), *How Stories Mean* (Erin, Ontario: Porcupine's Quill, 1993), p.189.

Chapter 5

1   'Labor Day Dinner', in Alice Munro, *The Moons of Jupiter* (Harmondsworth: Penguin, 1984), p. 150. All quotes will be taken from this edition and included in the text.

2   'Alice Munro Interview', in G. Hancock, *Canadian Writers at Work* (Toronto: Oxford University Press, 1987), p. 222.

3   See W. R. Martin, 'Hanging Pictures Together: *Something I've Been Meaning to Tell You*', in J. Miller (ed.), *The Art of Alice Munro: Saying the Unsayable* (Ontario: University of Waterloo Press, 1984), pp. 21–36; a similar point is made by Dennis Duffy in his review of *Alice Munro: Selected Stories*, *Books in Canada*, 125:9 (1996), 8–9.

4   For a history of the Janet Fleming character, see Helen Hoy, 'Rose and Janet: Alice Munro's Metafiction', *Canadian Literature*, 121 (Summer 1989), 58–93.

5   Martin, 'Hanging Pictures Together', p. 34.

6   Hancock interview, p. 201.

7   My analysis of story structure here owes much to the model proposed in 1989 by one of my undergraduate students, John Murphy, in an unpublished essay written for the Canadian Women's Writing course at the University of Reading. I am very grateful for his insights and diagrams.

8   'Layers of Life: Interview with Stephen Smith', *Quill & Quire* (August 1994), 240.

9   Abraham Edel, *Aristotle and His Philosophy* (London: Croom Helm, 1982), p. 92.

10 Gillian Beer, 'Beyond Determinism: George Eliot and Virginia Woolf', in Mary Jacobus (ed.), *Women Writing and Writing about Women* (London: Croom Helm, 1979), pp. 80–99.

11 Hancock interview, pp. 193–4.

12 Alicia Borinsky, 'Jean Rhys: Poses of a Woman as Guest', in S. R. Suleiman (ed.), *The Female Body in Western Culture* (Cambridge, Massachusetts: Harvard University Press, 1986), pp. 288–304.

13 The pattern of movement of Jupiter's satellites is not only extremely complex and so far incompletely mapped, but the number of 'moons' is being continually revised. In Munro's story first published 1978 she cites 'thirteen moons' and Janet's father remembers when two of these were discovered; in 1979 three more moons were discovered by US Voyager spacecraft, and with the 1995 Galileo space probe it is more than likely that our knowledge of this system will dramatically expand again. With this planetary system there remains always a sense of indeterminacy and mystery.

14 This story was first published two years after the death of Munro's own father during cardiac surgery. I am indebted to the chapter 'Grief and a Headhunter's Rage' in Renato Rosaldo, *Culture and Truth* (London and New York: Routledge, 1993) for some of the ideas on bereavement which I explore here.

15 For a feminist critique of the 'god tricks' of science, see H. J. Nast and A. Kobayashi, 'Re-Corporealizing Vision', in Nancy Duncan (ed.), *Body Space: Destabilizing Geographies of Gender and Sexuality* (London and New York: Routledge, 1996), pp. 75–93. By contrast, for a nineteenth-century woman's views on cosmology, see Linda E. Marshall, 'Astronomy of the Invisible: Contexts for Christina Rossetti's Heavenly Parables', *Women's Writing*, 2:2 (1995), 167–81.

16 James Carscallen, *The Other Country: Patterns in the Writing of Alice Munro* (Toronto: ECW Press, 1993), p. 471.

17 See James Gleick, *Chaos: Making a New Science* (London: Heinemann, 1988), p. 279.

Chapter 6

1   Trinh T. Minh-ha, *Woman, Native, Other: Writing Postcoloniality and Feminism* (Bloomington: Indiana University Press, 1989), p. 2.

2   Trinh T. Minh-ha in conversation with Annamaria Morelli, 'The Undone Interval', in Iain Chambers and Lidia Curti (eds), *The Post-Colonial Question; Common Skies, Divided Horizons* (London and New York: Routledge, 1996), pp. 3–17.

3   Michel Foucault, 'The Order of Discourse' in R. Young (ed.), *Untying the Text: A Post-Structuralist Reader* (London: Routledge, 1981), pp. 51–78; Trinh T. Minh-ha, 'The Undone Interval'; Patricia McKie, *Heroic Commitment in Richardson, Eliot and James* (Princeton: Princeton University Press, 1986), pp. 3–50.

4   Alice Munro, 'What is Real?', in J. Metcalf (ed.), *Making It New: Contemporary Canadian Stories* (Toronto: Methuen, 1982); repr. in J. Metcalf and J. R. (Tim) Struthers (eds), *How Stories Mean* (Erin, Ontario: Porcupine's Quill, 1993), pp. 331–4.

5   Alice Munro, *The Progress of Love* (London: Flamingo, 1988), p. 13. All quotes will be taken from this edition and included in the text.

6   John Donne, *Complete Poetry and Selected Prose*, ed. John Hayward (London: Nonesuch, 1967), pp. 93–96.

7   For an exploration of some of the multiple meanings coded into this rubbish heap, see Heliane Ventura, '"Fits": A Baroque Tale', *RANAM*, 22 (1989), 89–98.

8   'Atlamal in Groenlenzko', in *The Poetic Edda*, ed. Ursula Dronke (Oxford: Clarendon, 1969), vol. 1, pp. 77–97. I am grateful to my colleague David J. Williams for locating this quotation in *The Poetic Edda*, vol. 1, p. 82.

9   'Atlamal in Groenlenzko', in *The Poetic Edda*, stanza 9, ll. 7–8, vol. 1, p. 78.

10 The Alice Munro Papers, Accession #3, Special Collection/Archives, University of Calgary Library, now referred to as the Alice Munro fonds Accession no. 396/87.3. I wish to acknowledge the kindness of Apollonia Steele, Jean Tener and Jean Moore, custodians of the Alice Munro Papers, for making the uncollected materials of the Alice Munro Accession #3 available to me for initial perusal in August 1988 and for help in locating the updated catalogue version on Website address http://www.ucalgary.ca/library/SpecColl/munroa.htm> All references to drafts contain Box and File numbers from Accession 396/87.3.

11 Accession 396/87.3: Box 8. File 11.

12   Accession 396/87.3: 8.1 and 8.7.

13   Accession 396/87.3: 6.1. n. d.

14   Accession 396/87.3: 10.8. n. d.

15   Accession 396/87.3: 10.8. n. d.

16   Minh-ha, 'The Undone Interval', p. 8.

Chapter 7

1   Adrienne Rich, 'When We Dead Awaken: Writing as Re-Vision', in *On Lies, Secrets, and Silence: Selected Prose 1966–1978* (London: Virago, 1980), pp. 33–50.

2   Carol Shields, 'In Ontario' (Review of *Friend of My Youth*) in *London Review of Books* (7 February 1991), 22–3.

3   Rich, 'Foreword: On History, Illiteracy, Passivity, Violence, and Women's Culture', in *On Lies, Secrets, and Silence*, p. 12.

4   Magdalene Redekop, *Mothers and Other Clowns: The Stories of Alice Munro* (London and New York: Routledge, 1992), p. 209; P. Buitenhuis, 'The Wilds of the Past', *Books in Canada* (May 1990), 19–22; Eleanor Wachtel, 'Interview with Alice Munro', *Brick*, 40 (Winter 1991), 48–51.

5   Alice Munro, 'Friend of My Youth', in *Friend of My Youth* (London: Vintage, 1991), p. 26. All quotes will be taken from this edition and included in the text.

6   Redekop has researched Munro's own Scottish connections, and one of Munro's ancestors was James Hogg, author of *The Private Memoirs and Confessions of a Justified Sinner* (1824); see Redekop, 'Beyond Closure: Buried Alive with Hogg's *Justified Sinner*', *English Literary History*, 52:1 (1985), 159–84.

7   Shields, 'In Ontario', 22.

8   Carole Gerson, 'Anthologies and the Canon of Early Canadian Women Writers', in Lorraine McMullen (ed.), *Re (Dis)covering Our Foremothers* (Ottawa: University of Ottawa Press, 1990), pp. 55–76.

9   Mary Poovey, *The Proper Lady and the Woman Writer: Ideology as Style in the Works of Mary Wollstonecraft, Mary Shelley and Jane Austen* (Chicago and London: University of Chicago Press, 1984).

10   Claire Tomalin's review in *The Independent* (4 November 1990) is quoted in Redekop, *Mothers and Other Clowns*, p. 216.

11 I am very grateful to Patricia Hamilton, Curatorial Assistant, Goderich County Museum Archives, for making material about Eloise A. Skimings available to me on my visit in May 1995, and also to Dennis and Mary Ann Duffy who provided Skimings's obituary notice from *The Clinton News-Record* (14 April 1921). This raises the unanswered question, why did Munro cut off her poetess's life at 1904 and not allow her to survive till 1921?

12 For a reading which emphasises the metonymic connection between the onset of menses and Almeda's poetic conception, see Kathleen Wall, 'Representing the Body: Framing Narratives in Margaret Atwood's "Giving Birth" and Alice Munro's "Meneseteung"', *Canadian Literature*, 154 (1997), 74–90.

13 See Heather Murray, 'Women in the Wilderness', in S. Neuman and S. Kamboureli (eds), *A Mazing Space: Writing Canadian Women Writing* (Edmonton: Longspoon/NeWest, 1986), pp. 74–83; C. A. Howells, *Private and Fictional Words: Canadian Women Novelists of the 1970s and 1980s* (London and New York: Methuen, 1987) , pp. 11–16.

14 *The New Yorker* (January 11 1988), 28–38.

15 Heliane Ventura, '"Fits": A Baroque Tale', *RANAM*, 22 (1989), 89–98.

16 Rich, 'Women and Honor: Some Notes on Lying', in *On Lies, Secrets, and Silence*, pp. 187–94.

Chapter 8

1 Pleuke Boyce and Ron Smith, 'A National Treasure: Interview with Alice Munro', *Meanjin*, 54:2 (1995), 222–32.

2 Stephen Smith, 'Interview with Alice Munro,' *Quill & Quire* (August 1994), 1.

3 Boyce and Smith interview, 225.

4 See Ildiko de Papp Carrington, 'What's in a Title? Alice Munro's "Carried Away"', *Studies in Short Fiction*, 30:4 (1993), 55–64.

5 Boyce and Smith interview, 227.

6 Smith interview, 2.

7 For accounts of Munro's family background, see Catherine Sheldrick Ross, *Alice Munro: A Double Life* (Toronto: ECW Press, 1992); also Chris Gittings, 'Constructing a Scots–Canadian Ground:

History and Cultural Translation in Alice Munro', *Studies in Short Fiction*, 34:1 (Winter 1997) 27–37. I am also indebted to Gittings for information on the religious dimension of 'A Wilderness Station' and his comments on Munro's wilderness as geographical and spiritual landscape.

8   Elizabeth Heckendorn Cook, *Epistolary Bodies: Gender and Genre in the Eighteenth-Century Republic of Letters* (Stanford: Stanford University Press, 1996), p. 2.

9   C. A. Howells,'Writing Wilderness: Margaret Atwood's "Death by Landscape" and "Wilderness Tips"', in S. Chew and L. Hunter (eds), *Borderblur: Poetry and Poetics in Contemporary Canadian Literature* (Edinburgh: Quadriga Press, 1996), pp. 9–18.

10   George Woodcock, 'The Secrets of Her Success,' *Quill & Quire*, (August, 1994), 25.

11   Hayden White, 'The Historical Text as Literary Artifact', in R. H. Canary and H. Kozicki (eds), *The Writing of History: Literary Form and Historical Understanding* (Madison: University of Wisconsin Press, 1978), pp. 41–62.

12   Luce Irigaray, 'Questions', in *This Sex Which Is Not One*, trans. C. Porter with C. Burke (Ithaca: Cornell University Press, 1985), pp. 119–69.

13   For my discussion of Munro's earlier versions of female romantic fantasy in 'Baptizing', 'Simon's Luck' and 'Bardon Bus' see C. A. Howells, *Private and Fictional Words: Canadian Women Novelists of the 1970s and 1980s* (London and New York: Methuen, 1987), pp. 80–6.

14   Irigaray, 'Così fan Tutti', in *This Sex Which Is Not One*, p. 99.

15   Boyce and Smith interview, 227.

16   The version of this story in *The New Yorker* (19 July 1993), 62–70, avoids analysis of the dynamics of desire and its confrontation with reality by casting this whole section in the past tense.

17   Roland Barthes, 'The Third Meaning: Research Notes on some Eisenstein Stills', in Susan Sontag (ed.), *Barthes: Selected Writings* (Oxford: Fontana/Collins, 1983), pp. 317–32.

18   Irigaray, 'Così fan Tutti', p. 95.

19   Boyce and Smith interview, 227.

Chapter 9

1   James Wood, Review of *Alice Munro: Selected Stories, London Review of Books*, 19:9 (8 May 1997), 31–2.

2   Munro's stories have appeared *inter alia* in Margaret Atwood and Robert Weaver (eds), *The Oxford Book of Canadian Short Stories in English* (Toronto, Oxford and New York: Oxford University Press, 1986) and *The New Oxford Book of Canadian Short Stories in English* (Toronto, Oxford and New York: Oxford University Press, 1995); Hermione Lee (ed.), *The Secret Self: Short Stories by Women*, 2 vols (London: Everyman, 1987); John Thieme (ed.), *Arnold Anthology of Post-Colonial Literatures in English* (London: Arnold, 1996); S. Gilbert and S. Gubar (eds), *The Norton Anthology of Literature by Women: The Traditions in English*, 2nd edition (New York and London, 1996).

3   J. Metcalf, 'A Conversation with Alice Munro', *Journal of Canadian Fiction*, 1:4 (1972), 54–62; Graeme Gibson, 'Alice Munro', in *Eleven Canadian Novelists* (Toronto: Anansi, 1973), pp. 237–64; J. R. (Tim) Struthers, 'The Real Material: An Interview with Alice Munro', in Louis MacKendrick (ed.), *Probable Fictions: Alice Munro's Narrative Acts* (Toronto: ECW Press, 1983), pp. 5–36; Geoff Hancock, 'Interview with Alice Munro', *Canadian Fiction Magazine* 43 (1982), 74–114.

4   Metcalf interview, 61.

5   Gibson interview, p. 250.

6   Prior to the Waterloo conference, the only essay of note is Helen Hoy, 'Dull, Simple, Amazing and Unfathomable: Paradox and Double Vision in Alice Munro's Fiction', *Studies in Canadian Literature*, 5 (1980), 100–15.

7   H. Horwood, 'Interview with Alice Munro', in J. Miller (ed.), *The Art of Alice Munro: Saying the Unsayable* (Ontario: University of Waterloo, 1984), pp. 124–35.

8   W. R. Martin, 'Hanging Pictures Together: *Something I've Been Meaning to Tell You*', in J. Miller (ed.), *The Art of Alice Munro*, pp. 21–36

9   J. Carscallen, 'The Shining House: A Group of Stories', in J. Miller (ed.), *The Art of Alice Munro*, pp. 85–101.

10 J. R. (Tim) Struthers, 'Alice Munro's Fictive Imagination', in Miller (ed.), *The Art of Alice Munro*, pp. 103–12.

11 J. Gold, 'Our Feeling Exactly: The Writing of Alice Munro', in Miller (ed.), *The Art of Alice Munro*, pp. 1–20.

12 Godard, Barbara, 'Heirs of the Living Body: Alice Munro and the Question of a Female Aesthetic', in Miller (ed.), *The Art of Alice Munro*, pp. 43–71.

13 Godard, 'Heirs of the Living Body', p. 45.

14 J. F. Tener, 'The Invisible Iceberg', in Miller (ed.), *The Art of Alice Munro*, pp. 37–42. J. F. Tener is the archivist of the University of Calgary, which hold Munro's papers.

15 Web address: http://www.ucalgary.ca/library/SpecColl/munroa.htm.

16 Struthers, 'The Real Material', pp. 5–36.

17 R. Thacker '"Clear Jelly": Alice Munro's Narrative Dialectics', in Louis MacKendrick (ed.), *Probable Fictions*, pp. 37-60.

18 Catherine Sheldrick Ross, '"At Least Part Legend": the Fiction of Alice Munro', in MacKendrick (ed.), *Probable Fictions*, pp. 112–26.

19 Margaret Gail Osachoff, in MacKendrick (ed.), *Probable Fictions*, pp. 61–82.

20 L. Irvine, 'Changing is the Word I Want', in MacKendrick (ed.), *Probable Fictions*, pp. 99–111.

21 Irvine, 'Changing', p. 104.

22 R. Thacker's essay appears in K. P. Stich (ed.), *Reflections: Autobiography and Canadian Literature* (Ottawa: University of Ottawa Press, 1988), pp. 153–61.

23 Ildiko de Papp Carrington, *Controlling the Uncontrollable: The Fiction of Alice Munro* (Dekalb: N. Illinois University Press, 1989) p. 12.

24 Charles Forceville, 'Alice Munro's Layered Structures', in C. C. Barfoot and Theo D'Haen (eds), *Shades of Empire in Colonial and Post-Colonial Literatures* (Amsterdam: Rodopi, 1993), pp. 301–10.

25 Ajay Heble, *The Tumble of Reason: Alice Munro's Discourse of Absence* (Toronto: University of Toronto Press, 1994).

26 Heble, *Tumble of Reason*, p. 20.

27 James Carscallen, *The Other Country: Patterns in the Writing of Alice Munro* (Toronto: ECW Press, 1993), p. viii.

28 B. J. Rasporich, *Dance of the Sexes: Art and Gender in the Fiction of Alice Munro* (Edmonton: University of Alberta Press, 1990).

29 S. Kamboureli's essay in S. Neuman and S. Kamboureli (eds), *A Mazing Space: Writing Canadian Women's Writing* (Edmonton: Longspoon/NeWest, 1987), pp. 31–8.

30 Helen Hoy, 'Unforgettable, Indigestible Messages', *Journal of Canadian Studies*, 26:1 (1991), 5–26.

31   Magdalene Redekop, *Mothers and Other Clowns: The Stories of Alice Munro* (London and New York: Routledge, 1992), p. 239

32   A. E. Christa Canitz and R. Seamon, 'The Rhetoric of Fictional Realism in the Stories of Alice Munro', *Canadian Literature*, 150 (Autumn 1996), 67–80.

33   K. J. Mayberry, '"Every Last Thing … Everlasting": Alice Munro and the Limits of Narrative', *Studies in Short Fiction*, 29:4 (1992), 531–41.

34   K. J. Mayberry, 'Narrative Strategies of Liberation in Alice Munro', *Studies in Canadian Literature*, 19:2 (1994), 57–66.

35   Godard, 'Heirs of the Living Body', p. 64.

36   Alice Munro,'What Do You Want to Know For?', in Constance Rooke (ed.), *Writing Away: The PEN Canada Travel Anthology* (Toronto: McClelland and Stewart, 1994), pp. 203–20. The quotation appears on p. 218.

37   See Gillian Rose, *Feminism and Geography: The Limits of Geographical Knowledge* (Cambridge: Polity Press, 1993), Nancy Duncan (ed.), *Body Space: Destabilizing Geographies of Gender and Sexuality* (London and New York: Routledge, 1996); *London Journal of Canadian Studies: Special Issue on Geography, Gender and Identity in Canadian Literature*, 12 (1996).

38   'The Love of a Good Woman', *The New Yorker*: Double Fiction Issue, (December 23, 30, 1996), 102–39.

39   Alice Munro interview with Thomas Tausky, quoted in his 'Biocritical Essay', *The Alice Munro Papers: First Accession* (Calgary: University of Calgary Press, 1986), p. xvi.

40   Pleuke Boyce and Ron Smith, 'A National Treasure: Interview with Alice Munro', in *Meanjin*, 54:2 (1995) 222–32. The quotation appears on p. 227.

41   Full text in the Book of Common Prayer reads: 'But Thou, O Lord, have mercy upon us, miserable offenders. Spare thou them, O God, which confess their faults. Restore thou them that are penitent: According to thy promises declared unto mankind in Christ Jesus our Lord.'

42   'The Love of a Good Woman', p. 102. Munro's late story, 'The Children Stay', *The New Yorker*: Double Fiction Issue, December 22, 29, 1997), 91–103, also circles around female romantic fantasy, set this time in a small seaside town on Vancouver Island, British Columbia. I am grateful to Dennis and Mary Ann Duffy for showing me this story at a recent conference in India and for the

opportunity to share teaching a class on it in the Department of English, University of Pondicherry. Interestingly with Munro, there is always something more, or something else, which 'throws the story line open to question' *(BM*, 177).

Select bibliography

Primary sources

BOOKS BY ALICE MUNRO

Dance of the Happy Shades (1968), Harmondsworth: Penguin, 1983.

Lives of Girls and Women (1971), Harmondsworth: Penguin, 1982.

Something I've Been Meaning to Tell You (1974), Harmondsworth: Penguin, 1985.

Who Do You Think You Are? (1978) Published in Britain and USA under the title *The Beggar Maid: Stories of Flo and Rose*, Harmondsworth: Penguin, 1980.

The Moons of Jupiter (1982), Harmondsworth: Penguin, 1984.

The Progress of Love (1986), London: Flamingo, 1988.

Friend of My Youth (1990), London: Vintage, 1991.

Open Secrets (1994), London: Vintage, 1995.

Alice Munro: Selected Stories (1996), London: Vintage, 1997.

UNCOLLECTED STORIES AND ESSAYS

'What Is Real?' (1982), in J. Metcalf (ed.), *Making It New: Contemporary Canadian Stories*, Toronto: Methuen, pp. 223–6. Reprinted in J. Metcalf and J. R. (Tim) Struthers (eds) (1993), *How Stories Mean*, Erin, Ontario: Porcupine's Quill, pp. 331–4.

'What Do You Want to Know For?' (1994), in Constance Rooke (ed.), *Writing Away: The PEN Canada Travel Anthology*, Toronto: McClelland and Stewart, pp. 203–20.

'The Love of a Good Woman' (1996), *The New Yorker*: Double Fiction Issue (December 23, 30), 102–39.

'The Children Stay' (1997), *The New Yorker*: Double Fiction Issue (December 22, 29), 91–103.

Steele, A. and J. F. Tener (eds) (1986, 1987), *The Alice Munro Papers, First and Second Accessions*, Calgary: University of Calgary Press.

Secondary sources and interviews

Barnes, T. J. and J. S. Duncan (eds) (1982), *Writing Worlds: Discourse, Text and Metaphor in the Representation of Landscape*, London and New York: Routledge.

Barthes, Roland (1993), *Camera Lucida: Reflections on Photography*, trans. R. Howard, London: Vintage.

Beran, Carol L. (1990), 'Images of Women's Power in Contemporary Canadian Fiction by Women', *Studies in Canadian Literature* 15:2, 55–76.

Besner, Neil (1990), *Introducing Alice Munro's Lives of Girls and Women: A Reader's Guide*, Toronto:ECW Press, Canadian Fiction Studies 8.

Birkett, J. and E. Harvey (eds) (1991), *Determined Women: Studies in the Construction of the Female Subject, 1900–1990*, London: Macmillan.

Borinsky, Alicia (1985), 'Jean Rhys: Poses of a Woman as Guest', in Susan R. Suleiman (ed.), *The Female Body in Western Culture*, Massachusetts and London: Harvard University Press, 288–304.

Canitz, A. E. Christa and Roger Seamon (1996), 'The Rhetoric of Fictional Realism in the Stories of Alice Munro', *Canadian Literature*, 150, 67–80.

Carrington, Ildiko de Papp (1989), *Controlling the Uncontrollable: The Fiction of Alice Munro*, Dekalb: N. Illinois University Press.

— (1993), 'What's in a Title? Alice Munro's "Carried Away"', *Studies in Short Fiction*, 30:4, 55–64.

— (1994), 'Talking Dirty: Alice Munro's "Open Secrets" and John Steinbeck's *Of Mice and Men*', *Studies in Short Fiction*, 31:4, 595–606.

Carscallen, James (1993), *The Other Country: Patterns in the Writing of Alice Munro*, Toronto: ECW Press.

Chambers, Iain and Lidia Curti (eds) (1996), *The Post-Colonial Question: Common Skies, Divided Horizons*. London: Routledge.

Chew, S. and L. Hunter (eds) (1996), *Borderblur: Poetry and Poetics in Contemporary Canadian Literature*, Edinburgh: Quadriga.

Cook, Elizabeth Heckendorn (1996), *Epistolary Bodies: Gender and Genre in the Eighteenth-Century Republic of Letters*, Stanford: Stanford University Press.

Crouse, David (1995), 'Resisting Reduction: Closure in Richard Ford's *Rock Springs* and Alice Munro's *Friend of My Youth*', *Canadian Literature*, 146, 51–64.

Dahlie, Hallvard (1993), *Alice Munro*, Toronto: ECW Press.

Dronke, Ursula (ed.) (1969), *The Poetic Edda*, Oxford: Clarendon.

Diprose, R. and R. Ferrell (eds) (1991), *Cartographies: Poststructuralism and the Mapping of Bodies and Spaces*, St Leonards, New South Wales: Allen and Unwin.

Duncan, Nancy (ed.) (1996), *Body Space: Destabilizing Geographies of Gender and Sexuality*, London and New York: Routledge.

Edel, Abraham (1982), *Aristotle and His Philosophy*, London: Croom Helm.

Epperly, Elizabeth R. (1992), *The Fragrance of Sweet Grass: L. M. Montgomery's Heroines and the Pursuit of Romance*, Toronto: University of Toronto Press.

Forceville, Charles (1993), 'Alice Munro's Layered Structures', in C. C. Barfoot and Theo D'Haen (eds), *Shades of Empire in Colonial and Post-Colonial Literatures*, Amsterdam: Rodopi, pp. 301–10.

Gibson, Graeme (1973), *Eleven Canadian Novelists*, Toronto: Anansi.

Gittings, Christopher (1997), 'Constructing a Scots–Canadian Ground: History and Cultural Translation in Alice Munro', *Studies in Short Fiction*, 34:1 (Winter 1997), 27–37.

Godard, Barbara (1984), 'Heirs of the Living Body: Alice Munro and the Question of Female Aesthetics', in J. Miller (ed.), *The Art of Alice Munro: Saying the Unsayable*, Waterloo, Ontario: University of Waterloo Press, pp. 43–71.

Hancock, Geoff (1982), 'Interview with Alice Munro', *Canadian Fiction Magazine*, 42, 74–114. Reprinted in (1987) *Canadian Writers at Work: Interviews with Geoff Hancock*, Toronto: Oxford University Press.

Harris, Margaret (1986), 'Authors and Authority in *Lives of Girls and Women*', *Sydney Studies in English*, 12, 101–13.

Heble, Ajay (1994), *The Tumble of Reason: Alice Munro's Discourse of Absence*, Toronto: University of Toronto Press.

Hite, Molly (1989), *The Other Side of the Story: Structures and Strategies of Contemporary Feminist Narrative*, Ithaca and London: Cornell University Press.

Houston, Pam (1992), 'A Hopeful Sign: the Making of Metonymic Meaning in Munro's "Meneseteung"', *The Kenyon Review*, 14:4, 79–92.

Howells, Coral Ann (1985), 'Worlds Alongside: Contradictory Discourses in Alice Munro and Margaret Atwood', in R. Nischik and R. Kroetsch (eds), *Gaining Ground*, Edmonton: NeWest, pp. 121–36.

— (1987), *Private and Fictional Words: Canadian Women Novelists of the 1970s and 1980s*, London and New York: Methuen.

Howells, C. A. and L. Hunter (eds) (1991), *Narrative Strategies in Canadian Literature*, Milton Keynes: Open University Press.

Hoy, Helen (1980), 'Dull, Simple, Amazing and Unfathomable: Paradox and Double Vision in Alice Munro's Fiction', in *Studies in Canadian Literature*, 5, 100–15.

— (1989), 'Rose and Janet: Alice Munro's metafiction', *Canadian Literature*, 121, 59–83.

— (1991), 'Unforgettable, Indigestible Messages', *Journal of Canadian Studies*, 26:1, 5–26.

Irigaray, Luce (1985), *This Sex Which Is Not One*, trans. C. Porter with C. Burke, Ithaca: Cornell University Press.

— (1993), *Je, tu, nous: Toward a Culture of Difference*, trans. A. Martin, New York and London: Routledge.

Irvine, Lorna (1986), *Sub/Version*, Toronto: ECW Press.

Jacobus, M. (ed.) (1979), *Women Writing and Writing about Women*, London: Croom Helm.

Kamboureli, Smaro (1986), 'The Body as Audience and Performance in the Writing of Alice Munro', in S. Neuman and S. Kamboureli (eds), *A Mazing Space: Writing Canadian Women Writing*, Edmonton: Longspoon/NeWest, pp. 31–38.

McCarthy, Dermot (1994), 'The Woman Out Back: Alice Munro's "Meneseteung"', *Studies in Canadian Literature*, 19:1, 1–19.

MacKendrick, Louis K. (ed.) (1983), *Probable Fictions: Alice Munro's Narrative Acts*, Toronto: ECW Press.

— (1993), *Some Other Reality: Alice Munro's Something I've Been Meaning to Tell You*, Toronto: ECW Press. Canadian Fiction Studies 25.

McKie, Patricia (1986), *Heroic Commitment in Richardson, Eliot and James*, Princeton: Princeton University Press.

McMullen, Lorraine (ed.) (1990), *Re(Dis)covering Our Foremothers: Nineteenth-Century Canadian Women Writers*, Ottawa: University of Ottawa Press.

Man, Paul de (1979), 'Autobiography as Defacement', *Modern Language Notes*, 94, 931–55.

Martin, W. R. (1987), *Alice Munro: Paradox and Parallel*, Edmonton: University of Alberta Press.

Mayberry, Katherine J. (1992), 'Every Last Thing … Everlasting: Alice Munro and the Limits of Narrative', *Studies in Short Fiction*, 29:4, 531–41.

— (1994), 'Narrative Strategies of Liberation in Alice Munro', *Studies in Canadian Literature*, 19:2, 57–66.

Metcalf, John (1972), 'A Conversation with Alice Munro', *Journal of Canadian Fiction*, 1:4, 54–62.

Metcalf, John and J. R. (Tim) Struthers (eds) (1993), *How Stories Mean*, Erin, Ontario: Porcupine's Quill.

Miller, Judith (ed.) (1984), *The Art of Alice Munro: Saying the Unsayable*, Waterloo, Ontario: University of Waterloo Press.

Minh-ha, Trinh T. (1989), *Woman, Native, Other: Writing Postcoloniality and Feminism*, Bloomington: Indiana University Press.

— (1996), 'The Undone Interval', in I. Chambers and L. Curti (eds) *The Post-Colonial Question: Common Skies, Divided Horizons*, London and New York: Routledge, pp. 3–17.

Moi, Toril (1985), *Sexual/Textual Politics*, London: Routledge.

Neuman, S. and S. Kamboureli (eds) (1986), *A Mazing Space: Writing Canadian Women Writing*, Edmonton: Longspoon/NeWest.

Noonan, Gerald (1989), 'Alice Munro's Short Stories and the Art-That-Distrusts-Art', in J. Bardolph (ed.), *Short Fiction in the New Literatures in English*, Nice: Faculté des Lettres et Sciences Humaines de Nice, 141–46.

Poovey, Mary (1984), *The Proper Lady and the Woman Writer: Ideology as Style in the Works of Mary Wollstonecraft, Mary Shelley and Jane Austen*, Chicago and London: University of Chicago Press.

Radford, Jean (ed.) (1986), *The Progress of Romance: The Politics of Popular Fiction*, London and New York: Routledge.

Radway, Janice (1984), *Reading the Romance: Women, Patriarchy and Popular Literature*, Chapel Hill and London: University of North Carolina Press.

Rasporich, Beverley (1990), *Dance of the Sexes: Art and Gender in the Fiction of Alice Munro*, Edmonton: University of Alberta Press.

Redekop, Magdalene (1992), *Mothers and Other Clowns: The Stories of Alice Munro*, London and New York: Routledge.

Rich, Adrienne (1980), *On Lies, Secrets, and Silence: Selected Critical Prose 1966–1978*, London: Virago.

Rosaldo, Renato (1993), *Culture and Truth: The Remaking of Social Analysis*, London: Routledge.

Ross, Catherine Sheldrick (1979), 'Calling Back the Ghost of the Old-Time Heroine: Duncan, Montgomery, Atwood, Laurence and Munro', *Studies in Canadian Literature* , 4:1, 43–58.

— (1992), *Alice Munro: A Double Life*, Toronto: ECW Press.

Sedgwick, Eve Kosofsky (1986), *The Coherence of Gothic Conventions*, New York and London: Methuen.

Smythe, Karen E. (1992), *Figuring Grief: Gallant, Munro, and the Poetics of Elegy*, Montreal and Kingston: McGill Queens University Press.

Snitow, A. , C. Stansell and S. Thompson (eds) (1984), *Desire: The Politics of Sexuality*, London: Virago.

Somacarrera, Pilar (1996), 'Exploring the Impenetrability of Narrative: a Study of Linguistic Modality in Alice Munro's Early Fiction', *Studies in Canadian Literature*, 21:1, 79–91.

Suleiman, Susan R. (ed.), (1985), *The Female Body in Western Culture: Contemporary Perspectives*, Massachusetts and London: Harvard University Press.

Thacker Robert (1984), 'Connection: Alice Munro and Ontario', *American Review of Canadian Studies*, 14:2, 213–25.

— (1988), 'So Shocking a Verdict in Real Life: Autobiography in Alice Munro's Stories', in K. P. Stich (ed.), *Reflections: Autobiography and Canadian Literature*, Ottawa: University of Ottawa Press, pp. 153–62.

— (1994), 'Alice Munro's Willa Cather', *Canadian Literature*, 134, 42–57.

Tausky, Thomas E. (1986), 'Biocritical Essay', in A. Steele and J. Tener (eds), *The Alice Munro Papers: First Accession*, Calgary: University of Calgary Press, ix–xxiv.

Thomas, Sue (1995), 'Reading Female Sexual Desire in Alice Munro's *Lives of Girls and Women*', *Studies in Contemporary Fiction*, 36:2, 107–20.

Van Herk, Aritha (1992), *A Frozen Tongue*, Sydney: Dangaroo.

Ventura, Heliane (1989), '"Fits": A Baroque Tale', *RANAM*, 22, 89–98.

— (1992), 'Alice Munro's "Boys and Girls": Mapping out Boundaries', *Commonwealth: Essays and Studies*, 15:1, 80–87.

Wachtel, Eleanor (1991), 'Interview with Alice Munro', *Brick*, 48–53.

Wall, Kathleen (1997), 'Representing the Body: Frame Narratives in Margaret Atwood's "Giving Birth" and Alice Munro's "Meneseteung"', *Canadian Literature*, 154 (Autumn 1997), 74–90.

Weedon, Chris (1987), *Feminist Practice and Poststructuralist Theory*, Oxford: Blackwell.

White, Hayden (1978), 'The Historical Text as Literary Artifact', in R. H. Canary and H. Kozicki (eds), *The Writing of History: Literary Form and Historical Understanding*, Madison: University of Wisconsin Press, pp. 41–62.

Weinhouse, Linda (1995), 'Alice Munro: "Hard-luck Stories" or There is No Sexual Relation', *Studies in Contemporary Fiction*, 36:2, 121–29.

Welty, Eudora (1978), *Collected Stories*, New York and London: Harcourt Brace.

Whitford, Margaret (ed.) (1991), *The Irigaray Reader*, Oxford: Blackwell.

Williams, David (1991), *Confessional Fictions: A Portrait of the Artist in the Canadian Novel*, Toronto: University of Toronto Press.

York, Lorraine M. (1987), 'The Rival Bards: Alice Munro's *Lives of Girls and Women* and Victorian poetry', *Canadian Literature*, 112, 211–216.

— (1988), *The Other Side of Dailiness: Photography in the Works of Alice Munro, Timothy Findley, Michael Ondaatje and Margaret Laurence*, Toronto: ECW Press.

Young, Robert (ed.) (1981), *Untying the Text: A Post-Structuralist Reader*, London: Routledge.

Index